GOLDEN HART GUIDES
HISTORIC ENGLISH INNS

GOLDEN HART GUIDES

Historic English Inns

A.W. Coysh

SIDGWICK & JACKSON LONDON
in association with Trusthouse Forte

Contents

Front cover photo: The Shakespeare,
Stratford-upon-Avon
Back cover photo: Burford Bridge
Hotel, Box Hill
Frontispiece: Ye Old Mitre, London

Photographs by the British Tourist
Authority with the exception of the
front and back covers and ps 28,
34/35, 47, 48, 68/69, 73, 77 (THF); 49
(Andover Advertiser); 79 bottom
(Mermaid Hotel, Rye)

Compiled and designed by Paul Watkins
Editorial assistant: Andrew Franklin
Additional material: Dunja Hersak

First published in Great Britain 1983
by Sidgwick & Jackson in association
with Trusthouse Forte

ISBN 0-283-98915-7

Photoset by Robcroft Ltd, London WC1
Printed and bound in Great Britain
by Hazell Watson and Viney Limited,
Aylesbury, Bucks
for Sidgwick & Jackson Limited,
1 Tavistock Chambers, Bloomsbury Way,
London WC1A 2SG

Introduction The inn has played a significant part in English history. It has been a place where men have met to exchange news, to discuss their problems, to conduct business and to enjoy the company of friends. Whether it is known as an inn, an alehouse, a tavern or, more recently, as a hotel or public house, matters little; the distinctions have always been blurred, never more so than today. In this book the word 'inn' is regarded as all-embracing. It deals exclusively with the architecture, history and literary associations of our inns, for there are already many guides available for those who are primarily concerned about the facilities they provide.

The selection of inns has, inevitably, been a personal one, but an attempt has been made to present a fair cross-section from the humble public house to the 'grand' hotel and to cover a wide geographical field. Happily, there has been a renaissance of the English inn since World War II. They are fewer and better, and some owners have shown a real concern to conserve the traditions of the past while catering for the needs of the present.

Most people enjoy using old inns simply because they feel a vague sense of history. The pleasure can be greatly enhanced if the real facts are known. It adds something to a visit to know, as you park your car in a cobbled yard, that strolling players once performed Elizabethan dramas within its confines, or that you are drinking where Tom Paine formed the Headstrong Club, dining in the brewhouse of an ancient abbey, or sleeping, perhaps, where Charles Dickens worked over the plot of a novel, or where the friends of Charles II made plans for his escape to France. It is good to know these things, and if we bring an all-round connoisseurship to the way we use our inns, their best traditions will be preserved for future generations to enjoy.

The Inn in English Life

A Brief History

Many of our inns date back to medieval times. In those days travelling was hazardous; there were few roads worthy of the name and therefore few vehicles. Well-to-do travellers went on horseback, goods were carried by packhorse, and the poor, if they travelled at all, had to do so on foot. Those who did travel were mainly soldiers, merchants, or pilgrims anxious to visit the shrine of some saint, often in the hope that they might be cured of sickness or disability.

Monastic origins There were no inns as we know them today, but after the Norman Conquest every monastery founded a *hospitium* or hospice where callers could ask for a meal and to stay overnight. The monasteries had a rule of hospitality which laid down that all who called at the gate should be received and cared for. Those who could afford it would sometimes contribute to the maintenance of the hospice. There was usually a special hospice for the poor, often outside the monastery gates. Here food was served on a wooden plank or board on trestles, and pilgrims would sleep on a bed of rushes on the floor – they were literally given 'board and lodging'.

Many shrines attracted pilgrims, particularly in the south of England. Canterbury was always pre-eminent and after the murder of Becket in 1170 pilgrims flocked there in large numbers. Others were attracted to the shrine of Edward the Confessor at Westminster Abbey, to Christchurch Priory, to St Swithun's at Winchester, the Chapel of St Joseph of Arimathea at Glastonbury, and to Chichester,

Rochester, Salisbury or Gloucester. So many pilgrims came to the shrine of Edward II at Gloucester after his murder at Berkeley Castle in 1327 that a new hospice had to be built – now *The New Inn*.

Accommodation for pilgrims The wealthier pilgrims sometimes went to Rome or Jerusalem, embarking at Dover or Southampton on journeys taking many months. Special guest-houses were established in these ports where the pilgrims could wait for a good passage. The monks found running such a house a serious drain on their resources, for some of the wealthy lords expected high standards and in rough weather often stayed for days. Gervaise le Riche founded a God's House in Southampton in 1185 for pilgrims landing at the port on their way to Winchester or Canterbury. The pilgrimages reached their peak in the 13th and 14th centuries and continued into the 15th, though there was a decline after the Great Plague (1348-9).

Two crusading military orders were recognised as the guardians of the pilgrims and other travellers, and also of the sick and destitute. These were the Knights Templar and the Knights Hospitaller of the Order of St John. Both adopted an eight-pointed cross as their emblem and this later became one of the earliest inn signs. These orders established commanderies or preceptories, some of them small manor houses, where they worked under strict monastic rules. Many inn signs have their origin in these religious hospices: *The Salutation* and *The Angel*, for example, derive from the Salutation of the Virgin Mary by the Angel Gabriel.

It must not be thought that the Church alone catered for travellers. Many places had no hospice and the taverns and alehouses were able to some extent to meet the needs of wayfarers, though accommodation was often poor.

The Dissolution of the Monasteries in the 1530s brought a great change. The hospices began to disappear and their functions had to be taken over by others, usually the local lord of the manor or 'landlord'. (To this day an innkeeper is often referred to as 'the landlord' even though he may be a tenant.) Fortunately a few of the old guest-houses have survived as buildings – notably the *George and Pilgrims* at Glastonbury in Somerset and the *Angel and Royal* at Grantham in Lincolnshire. There are many other inns which incorporate parts of the old hospices.

Elizabethan inns By about 1590 the hospices had gone and inn-keeping became a private enterprise. Wealthy travellers would put up at the manor house and increasing numbers of taverns and ale-houses began to receive travellers. The lord of the manor would sometimes turn a smaller house he had vacated into an inn, or even erect a special building for the purpose. *The Spread Eagle* at Midhurst in Sussex is a good example of a manorial inn.

The Elizabethans were great travellers, stimulated no doubt by the example of their sovereign who sometimes stayed at inns – *The George* at Cranbrook in Kent, for example. Towards the end of the 16th century many new inns were built. Some of these had large courtyards surrounded by galleries with bedrooms. A gallery also formed a vantage point for patrons watching a performance by strolling players in the courtyard below. *The White Horse* at Romsey in Hampshire was built at this period on the site of the abbey guesthouse and the remains of the old gallery, now enclosed, may still be seen.

The 17th century By the beginning of the century the English inn was already well established. A great European traveller of this period, Fynes Moryson, tells us in his *Itinerary* (1617) that 'the world affords no such inns as England hath either for pleasure or cheap entertainment'. Nevertheless, there were many places that were still ill-served. At the end of the century Celia Fiennes, the noted traveller and writer, often had difficulty in finding a good lodging. Of a journey to Beverley in Humberside she wrote:

> . . . here we could get no accommodation at a Publick House, it being a sad poor thatched place and only two or three sorry Ale-houses, no lodgings but at the Hall House as it was called . . . being the Lord of the Mannours house.

During and after the Civil War period the serious shortage of small change made difficulties for shop-keepers and innkeepers. Between 1648 and 1673 many of them issued tokens for use locally. John Evelyn, the diarist, refers to 'the tokens which every tavern and tippling house presumed to stamp and utter for immediate exchange'. He goes on to say that these were only passable in the immediate neighbourhood, which seldom reached further than a street or two.

Coaching houses The urgent need for more provision for travellers came with the improvement of the roads which followed the first Turnpike Act in 1663, though the system did not spread rapidly until after 1710. The 18th century was a great period for inn building and particularly for the improvement and enlargement of existing inns. By 1770 the roads were very greatly improved and most of them were subject to tolls. They were crowded with traffic – coaches, post-chaises and horse-riders. The first mail coach completed the journey from London to Bristol in 1784. Horses could only be used over a limited distance and the inns had extensive stabling for horses which had to be changed at each 'stage' of the journey. Private carriages or post-chaises also changed their horses at the posting houses.

At this period many a Tudor inn was given a more pretentious Georgian frontage and often an assembly room. Such inns became important social centres, attracting the nobility and gentry, and innkeepers became people of importance, often members of the local council or corporation. Council meetings were often held at the inn and the refreshments taken became a charge on the rates. Magistrate's courts also used the inns and the assembly rooms were the scene of banquets, concerts and public meetings. *The Ship* at Brighton, *The Dolphin* at Southampton, and *The Lion* at Shrewsbury are examples of inns which played an important part in the social life of the day.

Early in the 19th century when the works of Thomas Telford and John Macadam produced still better road surfaces, traffic increased in volume and pace. Between 1803 and 1823 over 1000 miles of good roads were built, and by 1835 most main roads had been macadamised. This was the golden age of coaching and inn-keeping, but it was not to last for long.

In the 1830s competition from newly-built railways began to hit the coaching trade and, of course, the coaching inns. By 1845 most long distance passenger traffic had been captured by the train and many inns were sold. Some became local public houses; others private residences. Standards in general began to fall and in 1869 the Wine and Beerhouse Act gave local justices control over premises where liquor could be consumed, a power they retain to this day. Road traffic was mainly local, connecting towns and villages with the nearest railway station. Before the end of the 19th century the turnpike system was dead.

20th-century revival By this time, however, new mechanical methods of road transport had begun the great revival of the English inn. The first journey from London to Brighton had been made on a 'boneshaker' in 1869. Country inns began to cater for the touring cyclists, providing accommodation and meals. By 1937 The Cyclists' Touring Club had 4000 inns on their books carrying the club sign and providing bed and breakfast. *The Anchor Inn* at Ripley in Surrey became a mecca for cyclists and later for motorcyclists who rode down from London and back in the day.

After World War I, with the rapidly increasing popularity of the motor car, the revival of the English inn became certain. Some of the old coaching inns were restored, new inns were built and many sleazy public houses began to gain an aura of respectability. In the 1930s many roadhouses were built with swimming pools, dance halls and restaurants to attract young people from the nearest town – though few of these roadhouses have survived as such.

Post-war changes After World War II the major development was the growth of the motel or 'post house'. Although the number of licensed houses dropped by nearly one third between 1900 and 1970, more people used them and they became more respectable. At the same time the number of hotel and restaurant licences increased.

Increasing trade made it possible for the brewing companies and hotel chains which now own most of the old inns to make major 'improvements'. The more enlightened managed to retain the interesting architectural features of the old buildings or to restore them. Many of the old class-conscious Victorian bars were torn out and replaced by comfortable lounges.

The successful blending of old and new demands careful planning combined with a high order of workmanship. *The Hatchet Inn* at Bristol and the *Green Dragon Inn* at Lincoln show what can be done in urban surroundings. *The Swan* at Lavenham is a remarkable blend of restoration and rebuilding in a country town. One can only hope that the inevitable changes will not impair the character or destroy the atmosphere of our historic English inns.

Historic English Inns

*Asterisk indicates inns without accommodation. (THF) indicates a Trusthouse Forte Hotel: for worldwide reservations in any THF Hotel telephone (01) 567 3444

The Bull, Long Melford: carving

ALFRISTON East Sussex

*The Star Inn (THF)
High Street BN26 5TA
Tel (0323) 870495

One of the finest surviving examples of an old English hostelry, *The Star* was founded in the 13th c., probably as *The Star of Bethlehem*, and parts of the building date from *c.* 1450. It was built by the abbey of Battle as a hospice for pilgrims.

The late 15th-c. timbered frontage has an overhanging upper storey with three oriel windows, and the carved timbers show a figure in robes holding a globe in his right hand. His left hand is on his breast and a stag couchant at his feet. This is said to be St Julian, the friend of travellers. A pillar is carved with the de Echyngham family arms.

Above the doorway and below the centre window are two snakes, their tails entwined, supporting a niche. There is also a grotesque group with St Michael fighting an amphisbaena – a dragon or serpent with a forked tongue and with a second head on its tail. At the corner of the inn is a figurehead in the form of a red lion, said to have been taken from a Dutch vessel, possibly one of the De Ruyter's ships wrecked off Birling Gap, east of Cuckmere Haven, after the battle of Sole Bay in 1672.

The interior of *The Star* has massive moulded beams, chamfered joists and a stone fireplace, the cornice held by angel corbels. A wall-post bears the letters I.H.S. The bar to the right of the entrance was once the inn kitchen and has a fine early fireplace.

*Ye Olde Smuggler's Inn
(Market Cross Inn)
Waterloo Square BN26 5UE
Tel (0323) 870241

This 600-year-old building, black-beamed and now faced with white-washed tiles and weatherboarding, was once a large private house. Towards the end of the 18th c. it was the home of Stanton Collins, a noted smuggler – not that he needed to live a life of crime for he had respectable parents and was happily married. Nevertheless smuggling had a fascination for him and he led the Alfriston Gang, bringing contraband into Cuckmere Haven – a crime for which he was eventually hanged.

ALRESFORD Hampshire

The Swan
West Street SO24 9AD
Tel (096273) 2302

The inn is notable for its connection with the famous case of the Tichborne Claimant. The Tichborne estate near Alresford was managed by local solicitors whose chief clerk was Edward Rous. In the 1860s Rous became landlord of *The Swan*. On December 29 1866, a visitor registered in the name of Taylor and struck up a friendship with the landlord. Next day they drove together to Tichborne and Taylor talked much about the Tichborne family and local affairs. So much so that Rous began to think that Taylor must be none other than Roger Charles Tichborne, the heir to the Tichborne estate, despite the fact that it had been assumed that Roger had been lost at sea some years previously. Shortly afterwards Taylor was hailed by Lady Tichborne as her long lost son.

In 1868 Lady Tichborne died and Taylor became claimant to the estate. There were still some doubts about Taylor's identity and a Detective Wicher visited Alresford and convinced Rous that the claimant was in fact Arthur Orton and no relation to the Tichbornes. On February 1 1869 a meeting was held at *The Swan* at which the claimant successfully defended himself; Rous who had deserted him became so unpopular that he was forced to sell the hotel and leave the town.

Later, the claimant was arrested, imprisoned for over 50 days and then released on bail. When he expressed his intention of visiting Alresford the new owner of *The Swan* sent a decorated waggonette to fetch him and the claimant received a great reception from tenants of the estate who regarded him as their rightful landlord. In 1873, the claimant was forced to face a criminal trial and in 1874 was sentenced to 14 years penal servitude as an impostor.

AMESBURY Wiltshire

The George
High Street SP4 7ET
Tel (0980) 22108

Starting as a pilgrim's hospice attached to Amesbury Abbey, *The George* became a crown property under Henry VIII. General Fairfax used the inn in 1645 as a headquarters after he had succeeded Essex as commander of the Parliamentary forces.

In the 18th c. the inn was remodelled and became a halfway house for the Quicksilver Mail between London and Exeter. Some Dickens enthusiasts believe *The George* to be *The Blue Dragon* alehouse of *Martin Chuzzlewit*.

ANDOVER Hampshire

*The Angel
High Street SP10 2AR
Tel (0264) 2086

Originally *The College Inn*, this is the oldest inn in Andover, dating from the 12th c. King John stayed here when he gave the borough its charter in 1205. In 1435 *The College Inn* was destroyed by fire and rebuilt in 1444–5 by the owners, Winchester College, as a galleried inn. Traces of the old gallery may still be seen though it is now enclosed. The timber structure of the rest of the building is largely intact and the interior shows heavy beams supported by posts rising from a flagged floor.

The rebuilt inn eventually became *The Angel*. Its first royal visitor was Henry VII. In 1501 Catherine of Aragon stayed at *The Angel* when travelling from Plymouth to London. Richard Pope, grandfather of Alexander Pope, held the lease from 1582 to 1633. When his will was proved in 1633 it listed 26 rooms besides larders, cellars, barns, etc., each with its own name.

When James II was retreating from William of Orange in 1688 he took a meal at the inn with his son-in-law, Prince George of Denmark, and the Duke of Ormonde, who then left the king to his fate. *The Angel* was involved in the agricultural riots of 1830–1 when a mob invaded the town and the troops had to be called in when the local JP failed to pacify them.

*The George
High Street SP10 1NL
Tel (0264) 54592

An inn since 1576, *The George* is mainly remembered for a prosperous landlord called Sutton who wore a 'round-skirted sleeved fustian waistcoat, with a dirty white apron tied round his middle'. In 1826, when William Cobbett was making a speech about the Corn Laws in the inn, the audience were so interested, they failed to refill their tankards. Sutton accordingly tried to make things difficult for the speaker, but this so angered the audience that he narrowly escaped being thrown out of his own house.

The Star and Garter
High Street SP10 1NX
Tel (0264) 3332

There was an inn on the site in 1582 but the present building dates from 1827. It has three storeys with large bow windows on the first and second floors. A central portico with fluted Ionic pillars supports a railed balcony.

Charles I stayed at the inn in 1644 after a successful clash with Cromwell's troops and before proceeding to Whitchurch and Newbury. George III stayed at the inn on a number of occasions when travelling to Weymouth. In 1800 Lord Nelson stayed at the inn with Lady Hamilton and her mother.

The White Hart
Bridge Street SP10 1BH
Tel (0264) 52266

Dating from 1671, the inn was originally known as *The Lower Starre*. Andover was a very important centre for coach traffic in the 18th and early 19th c. and at this period *The White Hart* had stabling for 75 horses. After the decline in coach traffic there was a break in its history as an inn. In 1849 it was sold and became the workshop for a coachbuilder. It reopened as an inn in 1852.

ASHBOURNE Derbyshire

The Green Man
St John Street DE6 1GH
Tel (0335) 43861

This three-storey brick building is mainly Georgian. There is a large yard entrance from which a flight of steps leads to the dining room. During the 18th c. the magistrates of the Hundred of Low Peat met at the inn. At this time it was a centre for the sport of cockfighting. Dr Johnson and James Boswell stayed here several times and Boswell refers to it as 'very good' and to the mistress as a 'mighty civil gentlewoman'.

The full name of the hotel, *The Green Man and Black's Head Royal*, derives from the amalgamation of two inns, as seen from the fine gallows sign. On it rests the effigy of the 'Black's Head' and below swings a painted sign showing a forester wearing a green coat, standing with dog and gun. The 'Royal' was added after a visit by Queen Victoria.

AYLESBURY Buckinghamshire

The King's Head
Market Square HP20 1TA
Tel (0296) 5158

The timber-framed building dates from about 1450 and is approached through a cobbled way between shops. It almost certainly started as a hospice attached to the Greyfriars' monastery founded by Sir James Botelier in 1386.

Inside the inn is a fine hall in which the ceiling is supported by massive oak posts. The large mullioned contemporary wooden window contains lights, some with old heraldic stained glass. The first four shields have been damaged and are set back to front. The first shows the arms of England and France for Henry VI, and the fourth the arms of Anjou for Queen Margaret. The arms of their son who was killed at the Battle of Tewkesbury are also to be seen.

In the upper lights are the remains of a series of angels holding shields, the winged lion of St Mark with a scroll inscribed 'Marcus', original quarries with flower designs, the covered cup of the Boteliers (Butlers), and the chained swan of the de Bohuns. The Butlers, Earls of Ormonde, were lords of the manor of Aylesbury in the 14th and 15th c. The de Bohun chained swan has long been linked with the arms of Buckinghamshire. The hall contains many fine carved beams and the old wattle and daub wall construction is exposed in one place between the timber uprights.

The King's Head became an inn in the reign of Henry VIII, and the King is said to have stayed here during his courtship of Anne Boleyn, whose father was Lord of the Manor of Aylesbury. In the Civil War, Aylesbury was a Parliamentary stronghold and it was here that Cromwell received the thanks of Parliament at the end of the war in 1651. It is not surprising, therefore, to find that there is a bedroom at the inn where Cromwell slept, with a listening hole which enables the occupant to hear conversation in the hall below. In the 18th and 19th c., *The King's Head* became a coaching inn. The courtyard is still cobbled and the old wooden entrance gates are still in place.

BAGSHOT Surrey

Cricketers Hotel (THF)
London Road GU19 5HR
Tel (0276) 73196

The Cricketers stands on the site of a 17th-c. inn with extensive stabling and outbuildings. In front of it stood a turnpike gate, the toll-collector's cottage and a large pump for watering the road and supplying the inn. This was the main highway from London to Exeter, and as many as 30 coaches changed horses at Bagshot.

The property of the inn adjoins Bagshot Park, the former hunting grounds of James I and Charles I. Here on the park's estate lived the Duke of Connaught, whose visit to *The Cricketers* is marked by a beech tree planted by him on the lawn of the hotel on October 3, 1927. Apart from royal associations, Bagshot Heath was a dread haunt of highwaymen and it was near the inn that the last local robbery took place. Additionally, the inn itself has been linked to a ghost tale of 'Old John', whose visit was reported in the late 1840s and published by Lord John Newcastle in 1856 (*Authentic Ghost Tales*).

BARNARD CASTLE Durham

The King's Head
Market Place DL12 8ND
Tel (0833) 38356

Charles Dickens and Hablot Browne, his illustrator, stayed at the inn after coming by post chaise from *The Morritt Arms* at Greta Bridge on February 2 1838. Dickens was collecting material for *Nicholas Nickleby*. This part of the country was noted for its 'cheap' boarding schools and Dickens, anxious to see one, chose Bowes Academy, a school presided over by a man called William Shaw. To avoid suspicion he took an assumed name and presented a formal letter from a fictitious London solicitor explaining that he was acting for the widowed mother of a small boy who was considering sending the lad to a boarding school. Dickens saw the school and was horrified.

Looking across the road from the coffee room of *The Kings' Head* during his visit, Dickens saw a shop, with the sign 'Humphreys, Clockmaker' above the doorway. *Master Humphrey's Clock* became the title for a series of miscellaneous stories he projected, though the original idea was soon abandoned in favour of two full-length novels – *The Old Curiosity Shop* and *Barnaby Rudge* – which were issued in parts under this overall title.

BATH Avon

The Francis Hotel (THF)
Queen Square BA1 2HH
Tel (0225) 24257

The hotel consists of six Georgian houses (Nos 6–11), four of which were damaged in an air raid in April 1942 and were later carefully rebuilt in the same style. The square was designed by John Wood the Elder and built by Samuel Emes between 1729 and 1736.

Queen Square, named after George II's Queen Caroline, was the first of Bath's squares and a fashionable centre of private houses. Several of them have interesting associations. It is almost certain that John Wood the Elder lived and died in No 9. In 1799 Jane Austen lodged at No 13 with a Mrs Bromley who kept lodgings at Nos 12 and 13 adjoining *The Francis Hotel* on the west side. In July 1814, Harriet Westbrook, Shelley's wife, came to live at No 6 after her husband had eloped to the continent with Mary Godwin.

BATTLE East Sussex

The George
High Street TN33 0EA
Tel (04246) 4466

Built in the 18th c., the inn was designed to serve the increasing coach traffic through the town. In 1712 it was described as 'George with the gardens': these were hop gardens cultivated by the landlord who brewed his own beer. Public meetings were held in the inn from 1771; the magistrates' court met there from 1782 and during the Napoleonic Wars it became the military headquarters for the higher officers of the local command.

BEDFORD

The Bedford Swan
The Embankment, MK40 1RW
Tel (0234) 46565

Standing on the site of older inns, the present stone-faced building was designed by Henry Holland for the Duke of Bedford *c.* 1792–4. It has four storeys, the upper one with a pediment which spans the façade. The wide porch on four Ionic columns supports a balcony. The interior has a fine old staircase with twisted balusters dating from 1688, brought from Houghton House and installed in *The Swan* when it was built.

BEVERLEY North Humberside

The Beverley Arms (THF)
North Bar Within HU17 8DD
Tel (0482) 869241

Known in 1666 as *The Blue Bell*, it was rebuilt *c.* 1700 and again in the 1790s when the name was changed to *The Beverley Arms*. It is a three-storey brick building with a Tuscan porch surmounted by a balcony. In the 18th c. the inn had stabling for over a hundred horses. It was in the yard of the old *Blue Bell* that Dick Turpin was seen on a stolen black gelding in 1738. In 1737, after shooting Tom King in London, Turpin had fled to the East Riding of Yorkshire and set up as a horse dealer under the name of Palmer. In 1738 he was arrested on suspicion and the magistrates were prepared to dismiss the case. Further enquiries revealed his identity and he was convicted of horse stealing. He was hanged in York on April 10, 1739.

BINFIELD Berkshire

★The Stag and Hounds
Forest Road RG12 5HA
Tel (0344) 3553

This was probably at one time a hunting lodge in the centre of Windsor Forest. An old elm known as the 'centre elm', which has hidden many a miscreant, still stands on the old village green in front of the inn. In Elizabethan times the forest rangers and their families used the green for carnivals and Queen Elizabeth is said to have watched pole dancing from the inn windows.

In Georgian times *The Stag and Hounds* became a coaching house and during the Regency a new wing was built. William Cobbett spoke highly of the inn when on a journey from Kensington to Wokingham in 1822.

The interior is full of heavy oak beams, mainly original. In one door is an inset of decorated stained glass which was rescued from Westminster Chapel after the bombing of World War II.

BOLVENTOR Cornwall

Jamaica Inn
Bolventor PL15 7TS
Tel (056686) 250

The famous grey building of local stone and slate on Bodmin Moor was in existence in the 18th c. when it served travellers on the road to west Cornwall. It is known to have been called *Jamaica Inn* in the 1780s, possibly because of a traffic in rum. The inn served as a posting house for well over a hundred years but in 1893 for a short period became *Bolventor Temperance Hotel* before resuming its earlier functions. Bolventor was the setting for Daphne du Maurier's novel *Jamaica Inn*.

BOX HILL Surrey

Burford Bridge Hotel (THF)
Box Hill near Dorking RH5 6BT
Tel (0306) 884561

Burford Bridge was built in 1755 across the River Mole to take the expanding coach traffic bound for Brighton. As a result, a 17th-c. house close to the bridge was made into an inn – *The Fox and Hounds*. In the 19th c. this was enlarged and largely rebuilt to become *The Burford Bridge Hotel*. Its large garden with a fine box walk rises steeply to Box Hill (600ft), now National Trust property.

Many famous people have used the inn over the years. Lord Nelson stayed here with Emma Hamilton on several occasions. Keats completed *Endymion* at the inn – on the last page of the draft he wrote: 'Burford Bridge, Nov. 28 1817'. This was the culmination of seven months of concentrated work and he then stayed on for a while to rest.

Robert Louis Stevenson wrote parts of his *New Arabian Nights* at *The Burford Bridge* while on a visit when he formed a friendship with George Meredith who lived at Flint Cottage nearby. Many other writers used the inn – Richard Brinsley Sheridan, Robert Southey, William Wordsworth, and William Hazlitt who delighted to read under the shade of the apple tree in the garden.

BRAINTREE Essex

White Hart Hotel (THF)
Bocking End CM7 6AB
Tel (0376) 21401

The White Hart stands at the junction of two Roman roads where an inn is believed to have existed in Roman times. When the present inn first came into being is not known; however, county records refer to a 'Court held November 1 1591, in an upper room at ye signe of ye Hart in Bocking' (Bocking and Braintree were two separate parishes forming one town).

Most of the front block of the inn dates from this time, and although a good deal of alteration took place during the 1700s when *The White Hart* became a coaching and posting house, some fine 16th-c. timbers remain, especially in the bar and the lounge. The long iron bar in the ceiling of the archway entrance is a reminder of the custom of hanging meat and game in a place where a constant draught of air kept it in prime condition.

About 1830, part of one wing of the old building was pulled down to make way for the new assembly room and the news and reading rooms, which have been converted into the restaurant. As in the previous two centuries, here in the new building magistrates' and county courts continued to be held until at least 1852. With the advent of the railway *The White Hart* is reported to have retained its coaching and posting trade as late as 1889, when the inn's landlord still prided himself on being able to stable a hundred horses 'at a pinch'.

BRIDGWATER Somerset

The Royal Clarence
Cornhill TA6 3AT
Tel (0278) 55196

Built in the Regency style, *The Royal Clarence* was opened in 1825. It is a three-storey stuccoed building with a central portico supporting a balcony on four Ionic pillars. The arms of Bridgwater above the portico were brought from the old iron bridge over the River Parrett when it was demolished in 1883. Inside there is a fine assembly room with a musicians' gallery. *The Royal Clarence* was for some time an important posting house used by the Royal Mail.

BRIDPORT Dorset

The Bull
34 East Street DT6 3LF
Tel (0308) 22878.

This noted coaching inn dates from the 16th c. It was a stopping place for the Royal Mail from London to Exeter and Falmouth, the 'Celerity' from London to Exeter via Salisbury and Dorchester, the 'Eclipse' from London to Falmouth, and the 'Regulator' from London to Exeter. When the railway reached Bridport, *The Bull* ran its own coach to Lyme Regis.

The Greyhound Hotel
2 East Street DT6 3LF
Tel (0308) 22944

This 18th-c. inn was famous as a farmers' meeting place. A notice inside the yard entrance refers to the inn thus:

> *The place fixed for the delivery of the corn returns within this town is the Greyhound Hotel where an officer of customs and excise will attend as Inspector of Corn returns, to receive corn returns on the day on which such returns are required by law to be made.*

BRIGHTON East Sussex

The Old Ship
Kings Road BN1 1NR
Tel (0273) 29001

Facing the sea roughly midway between Brighton's two piers, the original inn on this site was owned *c.* 1670 by Captain Nicholas Tettersell who had carried Charles II across the English Channel to Fecamp in Normandy in a coal brig in 1651. It was rebuilt in 1755 and became the terminus for the London coaches and an important social centre in the town. Fanny Burney was invited to dine here in 1779 with Mr and Mrs Thrale in the officers' mess of the Sussex Militia. In 1789 a magnificent ball was held on the occasion of the birthday of the Prince of Wales. The prince, who was celebrating at the Pavilion, put in an appearance and joined in some of the dances. *The New Brighton Guide* of 1796 refers to a weekly ball and to the card assemblies on Wednesdays and Fridays. Mrs Fitzherbert was their patroness for a number of years but gave it up in 1830. Charles Dickens stayed at *The Old Ship* in 1841 when he was working on *Barnaby Rudge* and William Makepeace Thackeray worked in the hotel on *Vanity Fair.*

BRISTOL Avon

The Avon Gorge Hotel
(formerly *The Spa Hotel*)
Sion Hill, Clifton BS8 4LD
Tel (0272) 738955

The newspaper proprieter, George Newnes, built the hotel when constructing the hydraulic cliff railway from Hotwells Road to Sion Hill, now closed. He was given permission for the railway on condition that he revived the old Clifton spa by building a pump room at the end of Prince's Buildings. From the very beginning the enterprise was doomed to failure and the building became *The Spa Hotel*. The ornate building which once housed the mineral baths can still be seen with the initials G.N. in the masonry.

The Llandoger Trow, Bristol

*The Hatchet
Frogmore Street BS1 5NA
Tel (0272) 294118

Although probably the oldest building in the city, *The Hatchet* has undergone many changes and much restoration. The 16th-c. timbers, once covered with lath and plaster, have now been exposed and restored. Most of the old windows were replaced by sash windows in the 18th c. Early features inside include part of a staircase and a plaster ceiling on the first floor.

At one time *The Hatchet* was on the main road to Clifton (before Park Street existed) and for a period in the 19th c. it was frequented by prize-fighters including Thomas Cribb, Tom Sayers and Jem Mace.

*The Llandoger Trow
King Street BS1 4ER
Tel (0272) 20783

Originally consisting of five gabled private houses built in 1664, *The Llandoger Trow* was not made into an inn until the end of the 18th c. The name was that of a ship in which Captain Hawkins traded from the nearby quay.

Robert Louis Stevenson used *The Llandoger Trow* as the setting for the beginning of *Treasure Island*. Notable visitors to the inn were the actors and actresses who played at the Theatre Royal on the other side of the street, among them Sir Henry Irving, Wilson Barrett, Sir Herbert Beerbohm Tree and Kate Terry. The inn is now better known as a restaurant.

The Rummer
All Saints Lane BS1 1JH
Tel (0272) 22643

There was an inn on this site called *The Greene Lattis* in 1241. Then came *The Abyndon*, named after a noted musician. Later it became *The Jonas* and by the middle of the 16th c. *The New Star*. In the 18th c., known as *The Rummer Tavern*, it became an important coaching station with an entrance from the High Street. The front was rebuilt and a new approach made by John Wood the Elder

(1743) when he was engaged as architect for the building of the Bristol Corn Exchange. Many famous people have used *The Rummer* including Elizabeth I, Charles I, Charles II, William III and Oliver Cromwell.

BROADSTAIRS Kent

The Royal Albion Hotel
Albion Street CT10 1LU
Tel (0843) 68071

Overlooking the harbour, the hotel was completed in 1820 when it was known as *Ballard's*. The highest part has four storeys with a balcony at first-floor level. A dining room and lounge verandah extend on the seaward side from ground-floor level. The hotel now incorporates several old houses, one of them a lodging house in which Charles Dickens stayed in 1839 and wrote the latter part of *Nicholas Nickleby*.

Dickens was greatly attracted to Broadstairs. He stayed in the Albion for periods in 1845, in 1849 when he wrote part of *David Copperfield*, and again in 1859 despite the fact that he had already described the town as having become 'far too noisy'.

BROADWAY Worcestershire

The Lygon Arms
High Street WR12 7DU
Tel (0386) 852255

The inn dates from 1530. Since then there have been changes and additions but this building of warm, brown stone with its four great gables, mullioned windows and towering chimneys, remains a superb example of Cotswold architecture. The Jacobean doorway was added by John and Ursula Treavis in 1620. Treavis was landlord from 1604 to 1641 and his name, with that of his wife, appears on the carved woodwork. He was also responsible for interior features including the stone fireplace and the plasterwork in the room which Cromwell is said to have used in 1651 before the Battle of Worcester.

In the 18th c. the inn flourished as a coaching house. It was still doing well when, between 1815 and 1820, it came into the hands of General Edward Lygon who served under Wellington at Waterloo. His butler took over the inn on the understanding that it should bear the general's name and from that time it has been known as *The Lygon Arms*. As the years went by and horsedrawn traffic declined, the inn also declined. The revival did not come until 1904 when, by good fortune, it was acquired by Sidney Bolton Russell, a connoisseur who not only restored the fabric but brought in fine period furniture appropriate to the setting.

BUCKDEN Cambridgeshire

The Lion (THF)
Great North Road PE18 9XA
Tel (0480) 810313

At various times the inn has also been known as *The Lion and Lamb*, *The Lamb and Flag*, or simply *The Lamb*. *The Lion* was adopted as its sign in the 1860s to commemorate its past association with the See of Lincoln, for it started as a guest house for the palace of Bishops of Lincoln. It was built *c*. 1490 and its religious origin is reflected in the 15th-c. ceiling of moulded oak beams in what was originally the hall of the medieval building. At the junction of the beams, in the middle of the ceiling, is a large central boss carved with the sacred symbol of the lamb and the words *Ecce Agnus Dei* (Behold the Lamb of God). Other survivals of the original building are to be seen but most of it disappeared in the 18th c. when changes were made to convert the inn into a posting house.

BUCKHURST HILL Essex

Roebuck Hotel (THF)
North End 1G9 5QY
Tel (01) 505 4636

This inn probably began as a humble alehouse by the side of a newly constructed road through Epping Forest in the 17th or early 18th c. There is a reference to it as *The Buck* in the 1752 publication of *The Trials of John Swan and Elizabeth Jeffries* and it also appears by that name on Cary's map of 1768.

The only remaining parts of the old house are those occupied by the saloon, the public bars, the storage rooms and the staff quarters. The rest of the building is a reconstruction of the 1890s. Prior to the reconstruction *The Roebuck* had extensive grounds at the back with tea gardens, while on the green in front swing boats, roundabouts and stalls were set up in the summer. In the mid-1800s the house was popular for private parties, trade dinners and beanfeasts, since it had many large rooms, the largest of which could accommodate over 300 people. Also at that time, the traditional Epping Hunt held on Easter Monday used to meet at the inn. This hunt, to which thousands of Londoners flocked, to eat and drink rather than to follow the stag, provided material for the humourous writers of the time. Although the tradition died out in the 1860s it was continued as a show for holiday-makers until 1882.

BUCKINGHAM

White Hart Hotel (THF)
Market Square MK18 1NL
Tel (02802) 2131

The White Hart is a building of the 18th and early 19th c. An older house, traced from title deeds to 1725, was destroyed in that same year by a fire which devastated the town. The present building has the character of a typical old coaching inn. Remains of extensive stabling can still be seen at the back. Also to the side of the yard once stood the inn's brew house. In one of the two wings which runs back from the main block of the building, there was the old market room, a gathering place for local farmers, who came to discuss their crops, displaying samples of corn and buying and selling over a friendly drink.

In Victorian days, some time after 1850, when *The White Hart*'s coaching trade came to an end and its posting trade was dwindling, the brick façade of the inn was plastered over and a porch was erected in place of the arched entrance to the yard, all in keeping with contemporary taste and the image of a 'family hotel.' Of the original interior features a bedroom on the first floor provides a fine example of mid-17th-c. fashion. Its walls are wainscotted from floor to ceiling in painted pine panels, there are deep window seats, a six-panelled door and a marble mantelpiece.

The White Hart and the town have always had a close association with the mansion at Stowe, the seat of the Marquesses and Dukes of Buckingham, whose coat of arms has been painted in the late Georgian period in the inn's dining room. Visitors to Stowe, now a public school, keep the inn as busy as they did in the past.

BUCKLER'S HARD Hampshire

The Master Builder's House
Buckler's Hard, Beaulieu SO4 7XB
Tel (059063) 253

This is the end house in a row of red-brick Georgian houses which run down to the 'hard' on the Beaulieu River, where many battleships and merchantmen were built in the 18th c. The most famous British shipbuilder of the period was Henry Adams who lived here. Between 1749 and his death in 1805 he was responsible for over 40 ships, among them the *Agamemnon* with 64 guns which was launched in 1781 and captained by Lord Nelson in 1783. Launching banquets were held in the Master Builder's House which was converted into a hotel in 1926.

BURY ST EDMUNDS Suffolk

The Angel
Angel Hill IP33 1LT
Tel (0284) 3926

Built as a hospice for the Abbey of St Edmunds in 1452, *The Angel* still has medieval cellars with arched vaulting. It

The Master Builder's House, Buckler's Hard

expanded in the 17th c. when Bury St Edmunds became a flourishing wool centre, and again when the coach route from London to Norwich became important. The present Georgian building dates from 1779. It has four storeys and steps lead to the entrance through a pillared portico surmounted by a balcony.

Charles Dickens immortalised *The Angel* in *The Pickwick Papers*. He knew the inn well, staying there when he was reporting the electoral campaign of 1835 and again when he gave readings in the town in 1859 and 1861. From the inn he wrote, 'Last night I read Copperfield at Bury St Edmunds to a very fine audience. I don't think a word – not to say an idea – was lost'. In 1963 *The Angel* incorporated the adjacent *St Edmunds Hotel*.

Suffolk Hotel (THF)
38 Buttermarket IP33 1OL
Tel (0284) 3995

On the site of *The Suffolk*, the Abbey of St Edmunds at Bury owned a house as early as 1295. Its function as an inn,

known then as *Le Greyhounde*, was first recorded in 1539 at the time the Abbey surrendered its properties to the crown. In later years *The Greyhound* was a prosperous coaching and posting house *en route* to London and Yarmouth. Then in the 1830s the change of the old inn's name to *The Suffolk Hotel* was accompanied by extensive reconstruction.

The present lounge occupies the site of the inn yard which was then entered from the Buttermarket through an archway now replaced by the main door. In subsequent years the façade continued to be changed, particularly with the renovation of the windows as seen in the addition of marble columns on the ground floor. Today some traces of a medieval building can still be found. In the cellars remains of flint walls patched with stone and Tudor brick have been uncovered. There is also a hidden room in the house, probably sealed up in the course of the 1830s reconstruction and rediscovered a century later when hot water pipes were being installed for the bedrooms.

CALNE Wiltshire

The Lansdowne Arms
The Strand SN11 0EH
Tel (0249) 812488

Founded in the 16th c. as *The Catherine Wheel*, the inn is mentioned in the borough records of 1582. The old inn was enlarged in the reign of George II when the coaching route to Bath via Calne was becoming popular.

The inn has a long frontage with 13 windows in each of its two storeys and an unbroken parapet which carries a lettered sign. The entrance to the old courtyard now forms the entrance hall. When viewed from the front, the oldest part of the building is to the left. This carries a huge barometer at first-floor level, the needle set by a small barometer (by Yeates of Dublin) in the room behind. The inn was named *The Lansdowne Arms* between 1824 and 1829 and remained part of the estate of the Lansdowne family of Bowood until 1925.

CAMBRIDGE

The Blue Boar (THF)
Trinity Street CB2 1TG
Tel (0223) 63121

The inn certainly existed in 1693 when, according to the parish records, the churchwardens of All Saints' spent two shillings 'for Beer at ye Blue Boar on Ye Queen's Birthday'.

In the 18th c. the inn became an important coaching centre. In 1798, the landlord, John Mound, who was the Bishop of Ely's former butler, advertised coaches departing for London, Sheffield, Birmingham, Ipswich and Norwich. Early in the 19th c. there was a major reconstruction and later the courtyard was covered in.

*The Eagle
Benet Street CB2 3QN
Tel (0223) 353782

Although the building dates from the early 17th c. the main architectural interest is in the Regency gallery (*c.* 1815) supported by iron pillars. It was in *The Eagle* that John Mortlock, 13 times mayor of Cambridge between 1784 and his death in 1816, an MP at the age of 29, the first man to found a bank in the town and the most influential citizen, established the Rutland Club. Here all the important townsmen who supported the Duke of Rutland's Whig policies were liberally entertained. The Duke represented the university in the House of Commons between 1774 and 1779. In the 18th and 19th c. *The Eagle* was an important coaching inn.

CANTERBURY Kent

The Falstaff
St Dunstans Street CT2 8AF
Tel (0227) 62138

Built in 1403 to provide hospitality for pilgrims who arrived at the city when the gates had been locked after curfew, the inn was then known as *The White Hart*. The building has a number of Tudor features; the two upper storeys overhang beneath a hipped tiled roof, but the lattice windows are probably 18th-c. Inside are fine moulded beams and some early panelling.

The name was changed to *The Falstaff* in 1783 and in the 19th c. a massive wrought iron bracket sign was erected. In 1863 the Canterbury Pavement Commissioners ordered the owner to have it removed but a compromise was reached and it is certainly the most impressive sign in Canterbury today.

CHARLTON Wiltshire

*The Charlton Cat
Charlton SN9 6EZ
Tel (098063) 230

The inn is associated with Stephen Duck, a farm labourer born in the village in 1705. He started work at 14 and married when he was 19 but, after bearing him three children, his wife died in 1730. Meanwhile, Duck had started to write poetry. Some of his poems were read to Queen Caroline at

Windsor in 1730 and three years later she made Duck a yeoman of the guard and put him in charge of a library at Richmond Park with a yearly pension. Shortly afterwards Duck married Mrs Sarah Big, housekeeper to Queen Caroline. In 1746 he was ordained and became vicar of Byfleet in Surrey.

Stephen Duck is remembered more for the royal patronage than for the quality of his poems. Jonathan Swift expressed a professional and contemporary view:

> From threshing corn he turns to thresh his brains,
>
> For which Her Majesty allows him gains,
>
> Tho' 'tis confessed that those who ever saw
>
> His poems think them all not worth a straw,
>
> Thrice happy Duck! Employed in threshing stubble,
>
> Thy toil is lessened, and thy profits double.

Unhappy in his second marriage and depressed by the reactions to his verse, Duck eventually left London in 1756 and set out for his native village which he failed to reach. He drowned himself in a stream near Reading and was buried in Sonning Churchyard.

One of his poems was inscribed to the Lord Palmerston of the day who gave the rent of some land and a cottage to provide an annual 'Duck Feast' at the village tavern. This is held every year at *The Charlton Cat* where there are still some Duck relics.

CHARMOUTH Dorset

The Queen's Armes
The Street DT6 6QF
Tel (0297) 60339

The Royal Commission on Historic Buildings describes the inn as 'an unusually complete example of a small Medieval House'. It is a long two-storey whitewashed building with a relatively modern slate roof. There is much original timbering and over the doorway the initials T.C. are carved in a stone span-

drel. These are thought to be the initials of Thomas Chard, one of the Abbots of Forde Abbey. If this is correct, the building must date from the late 15th c. It is said that Catherine of Aragon stayed at this inn in 1501 on her journey from Plymouth to marry Prince Arthur. There is much more definite evidence to connect King Charles II with the inn. After the Battle of Worcester in 1651 the defeated king travelled north and eventually turned south via Cirencester and Bristol, arriving at Trent House in Dorset where he hid for some days. Meanwhile Captain Ellesdon and Colonel Francis Wyndham journeyed to *The Queen's Armes* where they met Stephen Limbry who owned a coasting brig which was to take the king across the Channel. Arrangements were made for Charles to join them at the inn. Meanwhile, Mrs Limbry had become suspicious about the sudden journey to be undertaken by her husband and she locked him in her room, threatening to scream the place down if he insisted on carrying out his plan. Charles was forced to leave *The Queen's Armes* and strike inland, travelling eastwards towards Salisbury. Eventually he crossed the Channel from the coast of Sussex.

In the years that followed the Restoration, a chapel was set up within *The Queen's Armes* where nonconformists could worship in peace. John Brice and Bartholomew Westley (as the name was then spelt), the great-grandfather of Charles Wesley, are known to have preached in the inn.

CHELTENHAM Gloucestershire

The Queen's Hotel (THF)
Promenade GL50 1NN
Tel (0242) 514724

On the site of the Sherborne Spa, the building was erected in 1838 by the architect Robert William Jearrad who laid out the Lansdowne estate at Cheltenham. The building, of white stucco, is in style a replica of the Temple of Jupiter in Rome. It has four storeys and the façade a five-bay portico with massive Corinthian pillars which run through the three upper storeys and support a crowning pediment. This is flanked by two four-bay appendages. On the ground floor the windows have semi-circular heads and are set back in deep recesses so that, seen from a distance, there appears to be a long colonnade of rounded arches. Above the windows are embossed painted crowns with the monogram V.R.

Cheltenham developed rapidly as a spa after George III and his queen came to take the waters in 1788. The main development to cater for the increasing number of visitors was between 1820 and 1840. The famous Promenade dates from 1825 and *The Queen's Hotel* provided its climax in 1838.

CHERHILL Wiltshire

*The Black Horse
Cherhill, Calne SN11 8UT
Tel (0249) 813363

Built as a posting house between 1765 and 1768 by William Catchway, *The Black Horse* is a red-brick building with stone-mullioned windows. At one time it had its own brew house, but this was demolished in 1939.

Travellers using the inn in its early days were liable to be robbed at night by the Cherhill Gang. One of them used to set out on marauding expeditions in summer without a stitch of clothing; which not only frightened people but meant he was less likely to be recognised. In the days of the Marlborough sheep fairs, the drovers on the way with their flocks used *The Black Horse* as a resting place. The sheep were penned outside and the drovers slept in the bar.

CHICHESTER West Sussex

The Dolphin and Anchor (THF)
West Street PO19 1QE
Tel (0243) 785121

The building has a fine Georgian frontage with a lettered sign on the parapet which is surmounted by a gilded anchor. The full name results from the amalgamation of two adjoining hostelries in 1910. *The Dolphin*, which was the larger, was a centre for the Whigs and its fine assembly room is said to have been built by John Abel Smith MP as a meeting place for his supporters. *The Anchor* was the headquarters of the Tories. In the 17th c. both were flourishing posting and coffee houses.

A landlord of *The Dolphin*, James Ballard, was for a time Posting Master to Queen Victoria. His widow, who died in 1874, was the last person in Chichester to use a sedan chair.

CHIGWELL Essex

*Ye Olde King's Head
High Road IG7 6QA
Tel 01-500 2021

This is an Elizabethan half-timbered building of three storeys and many gables. There is a large oriel window on the second floor and latticed bays on the first floor. Elizabeth I is said to have stayed here for one night and the following morning to have stood on the mounting block by the door where she scuffed and boxed an unlucky page for some neglect of duty. At this period the Court of Attachments and the Verderers Courts met at the inn.

Charles Dickens knew 'this delicious old inn near the churchyard' extremely well with its 'overhanging stories, drowsy little panes of glass, and front bulging out and projecting over the pathway'. He made it *The Maypole* of *Barnaby Rudge*. The picture he gives in the novel is as he imagined the inn in 1775:

> . . . *an old building with more gable ends than a lazy man would care to count on a summer day; huge zig-zag chimneys out of which it seemed as though even the smoke could not choose but come in more than naturally fantastic shapes, imparted to it in its tortuous progress . . . Its windows were old diamond paned lattices, its floors were sunken and uneven, its ceilings blackened by the hand of time, and heavy with massive beams.*

CHIPPENHAM Wiltshire

The Angel
Market Place SN15 3HD
Tel (0249) 2615

Formerly known as *The Bull*, this was a Georgian coaching inn of three storeys surmounted by a balustrade. The porch, also with balustrade, is supported by Tuscan columns. Tobias Smollett tells us that Peregrine Pickle's mother served in *The Angel* as a chambermaid, so the inn must have flourished before 1751 when his novel was published. An issue of the *Bath Journal* in 1774 contains this notice from the proprietor:

> *It having been found that the other Inns were not sufficient for Properly Accommodating the Nobility and Gentry Travelling through this Town, occasioned by the great Increase thereof rising from the NEW ROAD THE ANGEL INN is just now fitted up in a neat and convenient Manner; where the Gentlemen and Ladies who will be so good as to use this House will meet with the most obliging Treatment and reasonable usage.*

In the parliamentary election of 1875, Sir John Neeld of Grittleton, who was a Conservative candidate, had his committee room at *The Angel*. When the result was declared in his favour there was a riot in the town and rowdy scenes outside the inn. Windows were broken and the landlord climbed to the top floor and threw bottles at the crowd.

CHIPPERFIELD Hertfordshire

The Two Brewers (THF)
The Common, Chipperfield
Kings Langley WD4 9BS
Tel (09277) 65266

In the 17th c. *The Two Brewers* was a village alehouse within the manor of King's Langley. Houses on either side have been added since World War II. The building is of brick with red-tiled roof and a plaster and colour-washed front to which bay windows have been added. The post sign on the green carries the picture of two men carrying a barrel of strong beer slung from a pole, the ends of which rest on their shoulders.

In the 19th c. the tavern became the training quarters for bare-fist fighters. Bob Fitzsimmons, Jem Mace (champion in 1861) and Tom Sayers (champion in 1857) sparred in the old club room behind the main building and took training runs round Chipperfield Common. In those days the inn had large stables as former landlords farmed the adjoining land and provided overnight accommodation for hunters brought from a distance to follow the local foxhounds.

CHIPPING NORTON Oxfordshire

The White Hart (THF)
High Street OX7 5AD
Tel (0608) 2572

The origins of the inn may well be in the 14th c. because the town was an important wool centre in the days of Richard II. The painted wall sign bears his badge. The oldest parts of the present stone-built inn are Tudor but the three-storey frontage of mellow stone dates from 1811. The original wings formed a galleried courtyard but although the stone stairs led to it may still be seen, the gallery has long since been enclosed. In one room there is floor-to-ceiling Elizabethan panelling and some Tudor fireplaces may be seen. Chipping Norton became an important coaching centre towards the end of the 18th c.; all the through coaches from London to Cheltenham or Worcester inned at *The White Hart*.

CLIFTON HAMPDEN Oxfordshire

The Barley Mow
Clifton Hampden
Abingdon OX14 3EH
Tel (086730) 7847

On the south bank of the Thames, in the parish of Long Wittenham, this old building of timber and thatch dates

The Barley Mow, Clifton Hampden

from 1350. The curved 'crucks' of the frame for the walls can still be seen at the gable end. The low timbered ceilings inside cause all but the very shortest customers to stoop.

It was from the windows of *The Barley Mow* that Jerome K. Jerome watched the river, and wrote much of his *Three Men in a Boat*.

CLOVELLY Devon

The New Inn
High Street EX39 5TQ
Tel (02373) 303

Steps in front of *The New Inn* descend to the harbour of this little fishing village. It is a typical North Devon building with grey tiles and white-washed walls. It rises from the cobbles as though it had always been fused into the rocky hillside, although it was largely rebuilt after World War I.

COBHAM Kent

★The Leather Bottle
The Street DA12 3BZ
Tel (0474) 814327

A 17th-c. half-timbered inn, noted for its associations with Charles Dickens. He knew it well and used it for a scene in *The Pickwick Papers*. Tracy Tupman fled to *The Leather Bottle* after he had been jilted by Rachael Wardle. In a letter to Mr Pickwick he wrote, 'Any letter addressed to me at the Leather Bottle, Cobham, Kent, will be forwarded, supposing I still exist'. After receiving the letter, Mr Pickwick set out for this 'clean and commodious village alehouse' with Winkle and Snodgrass and found Tracy Tupman consoling himself with bacon, roast fowl and ale. They all stayed the night and next day returned to London. In 1841 Dickens stayed overnight at *The Leather Bottle* with his biographer, John Forster.

COLCHESTER Essex

The Red Lion
High Street CO1 1DJ
Tel (0206) 77986

Ancient mosaic pavements were found during excavations of the yard in 1882 because *The Red Lion* is on the site of a Roman building. There is early 15th-c. masonry in the cellars and parts of the present building reveal the wattle and daub structure of 1470 when it was the private house of a wealthy burgess. The house became an inn early in the 16th c. when it was licensed as a 'wyn tavern' and considerable extensions were made. The frontage is timbered with projecting upper storeys and the woodwork is finely carved. There are traceried panels beneath the windows of the upper floors and the spandrels of the arched Tudor doorway have 15th-c. carving depicting St George and the Dragon. Inside there are massive moulded beams with carved brackets.

In 1648 when Colchester fell after a siege by the Parliamentarians, the Royalist garrison was rounded up by Thomas Fairfax in the yard of *The Red Lion* and the defending leaders, Sir George Lisle and Sir Charles Lucas, were taken out and shot. In the 18th c. the coaching trade flourished. In 1756 an express service to London was inaugurated at the inn. In the entrance to the yard, now covered in, is a rainwater head dated 1716, a range of brass service bells and a fine old Parliament clock.

*The Marquis of Granby
25 Norton Hill CO1 1EG
Tel (0206) 77630

Built in 1520, the inn has some particularly fine 16th-c. timbering in the east wing including a carved beam with stylised leaves and animals which rests on brackets with carved human figures. The inn was extensively restored in 1914. The Marquis of Granby appears on the building as a wall sign in a plaster cartouche. John Manners, Marquis of Granby, was the eldest son of the 3rd Duke of Rutland. He was British Commander-in-Chief in Germany during the Seven Years War (1756–63). One day the marquis was about to lead a cavalry charge against the enemy when his wig fell off. His aide-de-camp drew his attention to the fact. 'Damn the wig', cried the marquis, 'I can charge baldheaded.' He had a warm feeling towards the men under his command and many of his officers who were disabled were helped by the marquis to establish themselves as innkeepers. Hence the frequency of 'Marquis of Granby' inns.

COLNBROOK Buckinghamshire

The Ostrich Inn
High Street SL3 0JX
Tel (02812) 2628

The inn was founded as a hospice in 1106 by Milo Crispin, in trust to the Abbey of Abingdon, 'for the good of travellers'. The name is a corruption of the word 'hospice': earlier versions were *Ospringe*, *Ostridge* and *Oastriche*.

In the 13th c. Thomas Cole, a clothier from Reading, frequently stayed at the inn on his way to London. John Jarman the innkeeper, and his wife, who already had a reputation for stealing from guests, prepared a bed for Cole which could be tipped so that its occupant could slide through a trap door head first into a cauldron of hot liquid in the kitchen below. Three times the scheme misfired when Cole decided to change his plans at the last moment; the fourth time Cole died, but when his body was later found in the brook the culprits were traced and hanged.

King John is said to have stopped at *The Ostrich* on his way to Runnymede to sign the Magna Carta, and Jean Froissart, the medieval chronicler, tells us that ambassadors who had been to dine with Edward III 'after they departed lay the same night at Colnbrook'. When the Black Prince returned from Europe in 1355 with his prisoner King John of France, he is said to have been met by his father, Edward III, at *The Ostrich*. It was certainly a well-known inn where visitors to Windsor often called to clean up before proceeding to an audience.

The present *Ostrich*, which dates from the early 16th c., is built of timber and brick with a double gable and once had a galleried yard. Elizabeth I stayed here in 1558. In 1649 when Charles I had been taken to London to stand trial at Westminster Hall, Captain Fanshawe and John Dowcett were on their way to London to meet a messenger who was to bring them news of the king. Seeing a man riding west, they assumed him to be the messenger they were expecting. He asked Fanshawe and Dowcett to come with him to *The Ostrich Inn* and when the small party arrived the Royalists were overpowered and locked up as prisoners. Shortly afterwards, however, Lord Richmond arrived with a group of Royalist supporters, carrying the message. Realising what had happened he threatened to set fire to *The Ostrich*; there was a short but fierce fight, and Fanshawe and Dowcett were released.

CORFE CASTLE Dorset

The Greyhound
Corfe Castle BH20 5EH
Tel (0929) 480205

The inn is at the foot of the hill on which stand the ruins of Corfe Castle – one of the last Royalist strongholds during the Civil War. The inn is of whitewashed Purbeck stone with a slate roof carrying dormer windows. The entrance porch is pillared and supports a small room. Throughout the coaching era *The Greyhound* was a useful stop on the route to Swanage. Thomas Hardy knew the inn well. He used the name of Corvsgate for Corfe in his novels *Desperate Remedies* and *The Hand of Ethelberta*.

CORSHAM Wiltshire

The Methuen Arms
High Street SN13 0HB
Tel (0249) 712239

The inn has a Georgian façade with a pillared porch which dates from 1805, but behind this frontage is a Tudor building which became *The Red Lion c.* 1608. This was previously Wintners Court and belonged to the Nott family. In 1732 Elizabeth Webber, a widowed member of the family, became the owner and the inn then passed in turn to her daughter, Christian. Perhaps the initials and date, C.W. 1749, carved on a wall, date from her time. When she died, *The Red Lion* passed to the Methuen family. There was then more rebuilding (1805) and the sign was changed to bear the arms of Lord Methuen. The stone doorposts of the entrance carry the traditional chequers sign used by tavern-keepers who were also money-changers.

CRANBROOK Kent

The George
Stone Street TN17 3HE
Tel (0580) 713348

When Elizabeth I came to Cranbrook in 1575 to see the important local wool and weaving trade, the accommodation at the inn was regarded as fine enough to meet her needs. There is a story that she walked into the town along a mile of Kentish broadcloth.

The inn now shows little sign of its real age. The long frontage with a tile-hung second storey with delicate wrought-iron balcony, and the steeply pitched roof with dormer windows, date from late Georgian times when the house became an important coaching inn. Inside are heavy moulded beams, open fireplaces, and a fine early 18th c. balustered staircase.

The magistrates' court was held in an upper room of *The George* for about 300 years and did not move to new quarters until 1859.

CRAWLEY West Sussex

The George (THF)
High Street RH10 1BS
Tel (0293) 24215

Since Regency times the inn's gallows sign has been famous. It spans the High

Street. When the coaching trade flourished an extension to the inn was built on an island site in the middle of the main road and the sign was erected to link the two parts. The original building was a private house which became an inn in 1615. This is the date on a massive stone fireplace with fine moulding and sunk spandrels to be seen in the hall. The roof is of Horsham stone slabs but the front, which is tile-hung on the upper storey, is relatively late.

The George was a half-way house on the coaching route through Reigate which formed the Brighton Road. The Prince of Wales first changed horses here on a journey from Carlton House to Brighton in 1783 and later became a frequent visitor. In the 1850s as many as 50 coaches changed horses at *The George* every 24 hours. Even when the railway came the decline was relatively slow, for amateur coachmen and sportsmen still used the inn as a port of call on record-breaking runs.

The George was closely associated with prize fighters such as Tom Sayers

The George, Crawley

and Pedlar Palmer who took part in contests on Crawley Down, but rather more people will know it as the inn where Belcher trained boy Jim for his fight against Crab Wilson in Sir Arthur Conan Doyle's novel *Rodney Stone*.

DARTFORD Kent

The Royal Victoria and Bull
1 High Street DA1 1DU
Tel (0332) 23104

Originally a hospice attached to the Augustinian priory of St Mary and St Margaret, the inn was probably where Canterbury pilgrims journeying from London spent their first night. In 1508 the house is described in a rent roll of the priory lands as Le Hole Bole with a rent of 40 shillings (£2) a year. Part of the present building is Elizabethan, though portions of earlier walls may well have been incorporated.

The Bull was at one time a galleried inn with a large courtyard. Changes were made in the 18th c. when it became

a coaching inn and the fine Georgian façade with its high windows was built with a central portico which leads to the courtyard (now covered in). Remains of the old wooden galleries may still be seen.

An incident in 1775 concerned a doctor, John Parker, who, while seeking to evade his creditors, took refuge in *The Bull*. A certain Joseph Stackpole arrived at the inn with a bailiff who was told to take Parker and lock him up. Parker, in anger, threatened the bailiff with a pistol and one of his friends put out the lights. Stackpole went to the rescue but Parker's friends seized him, a carbine he was carrying exploded and Parker was killed. Was it by accident or intent? Stackpole faced a murder trial at Maidstone and it was two years before the case was settled: the court finally decided that Parker died as a result of an accident.

DEVIZES Wiltshire

The Bear
Market Place SN10 1HS
Tel (0380) 2444

By the end of the 16th c. *The Bear* was in existence: there is a record that a certain John Sawter applied for a licence in 1599. Some claim that Elizabeth I halted at the inn in 1574 when travelling from Bath to Lacock.

Traces of the old inn still exist, but the frontage is mainly Georgian. The right wing is the earlier and has the entrance, a porch supporting a bear holding a bunch of grapes. The name of the hotel extends as a lettered sign right across this part of the façade. The later wing to the left is of solid stone blocks.

The Bear was one of the most fashionable coaching inns of the 18th c. There were many notable landlords. In the early 18th c. the owner, John Watts, lived in the inn and acted as host. He sold it to John Child, a local grocer and brother of Sir Francis Child, a London banker. In 1754 *The Bear* was rented by John Turner, a Land Tax Receiver. Then came George Whatley. The most interesting tenant, however, was Thomas Lawrence who came to *The Bear* in 1772. He was the father of 16 children. Fanny Burney describes a 'long visit' she made with Mrs Thrale while the Lawrence family was at *The Bear*. They were particularly impressed by the son, Thomas:

> . . . a most lovely boy of ten years of age, who seems to be not merely the wonder of their family, but of the times, for his astonishing skill in drawing. They protest he has never had any instruction, yet showed us some of his productions that were really beautiful. We found that he had been taken to town, and that all the painters had been very kind to him, and Sir Joshua Reynolds had pronounced him, the mother said, the most promising genius he had ever met.

Very shortly after this the Lawrence family left *The Bear*, and in 1779 young Thomas Lawrence started to work at a studio in Bath and soon became the main support of the family. He was to become the greatest portrait painter of his time. In 1815 he was knighted and in 1820 became President of the Royal Academy.

Many 18th-c. notables used *The Bear*, including Jane Austen, Samuel Foote, David Garrick, Dr Johnson, Sir Joshua Reynolds, Richard Brinsley Sheridan, Sarah Siddons and John Wilkes. Royal visitors have included George III and Queen Charlotte who stayed on September 16 1789, King Edward VII as Prince of Wales when he visited Devizes in 1893 to review the Wiltshire Yeomanry, Prince Arthur of Connaught, and Prince Edward of Saxe Weimar.

DORCHESTER Dorset

The King's Arms
30 High East Street DT1 1HE
Tel (0305) 65353

Mentioned in an Assessment of 1737, by 1783 *The King's Arms* had become an established coaching inn on the London to Exeter Road. It was here that George III changed horses when passing through Dorchester on his way to Melcombe Regis, or Weymouth, as we know it today. The three-storey frontage has two large semi-circular bays above a pillared portico and to the left is the arched entrance to the yard with a balcony on the first floor above.

The King's Arms has had many notable visitors. Admiral Lord Nelson and Sir Thomas Masterman Hardy, Kitchener of Khartoum, and, of course, Thomas Hardy who used the hotel lounge as the scene for the entertainment given by Michael Henchard, the Mayor of Casterbridge, to his friends.

DORCHESTER-ON-THAMES
Oxfordshire

The George
High Street OX9 8HJ
Tel (0865) 340404

Dorchester was an important centre in Roman times and from the 7th c. to the 9th c. was the cathedral city of Wessex and later of Mercia. The great abbey church (founded as a priory in 1140) still dominates the town. *The George*, which lies opposite the abbey, was once its hospice and dates, in part, from 1450.

In the 18th c. it became a coaching house on the London to Oxford route. The building retains many historic features. Behind the inn can be seen the old galleried 'lodgings' reached by a staircase, perhaps the earliest of its kind in the country. Many of the rooms are timbered and the dining room with its great fireplace is very little changed since it was the monks' brew house.

DORKING Surrey

The White Horse (THF)
High Street RH4 1BE
Tel (0306) 881138

This is a two-storey black and white building with a long frontage broken by three gables and a central coaching entrance. The oldest parts are 16th-c. but the origins of the inn are 13th-c. A building on the site was granted to the Knights Templar by William Warenne, Earl of Surrey, and later, in 1278, it passed into the holding of the Knights Hospitaller of St John of Jerusalem. The badge of the Templars was a white cross and the house was known as Cross House. The present name – *White Horse* – probably derives from White Cross.

The oldest part of the present timbered building dates from *c.* 1520 when it was used as a vicarage. In 1531 it was surrendered to George Rolle, gentleman, and was known as Rolle's Tenement until it became *The White Horse Inn* in 1750. Much rebuilding was done to meet the needs of the coaching trade. In the 1830s the landlord was William Penn, who claimed descent from the founder of Pennsylvania. At this period the inn became a favourite resort of invalids in the summer season.

DUNSTER Somerset

The Luttrell Arms (THF)
High Street TA22 6SG
Tel (064382) 555

The inn is said to have been a guest house of the abbots of Cleeve whose Cistercian monastery, now in ruins, is about 4m distant. It is a three-storey stone structure with a porch tower that was either built or materially altered between 1622 and 1629. The core is a 15th-c. Gothic hall, now divided by a floor into two parts. The upper chamber contains a fine hammer-beam roof, and the lower chamber, once the inn kitchen, is now a bar.

The building is known to have been an inn called *The Ship* in 1651. By that time the influence of the Luttrell family had manifested itself. Some of the rooms contain 17th-c. plaster work. The finest example is a tall overmantel which carries the arms of England and France and a panel showing Actaeon in the form of a stag being torn to pieces by his hounds on Mount Cithaeron. A male figure in a triangle may represent James I or the lord of the castle – George Luttrell. *The Ship* became *The Luttrell Arms* in 1779 in compliment to Hugh Luttrell whose family had been the lords of the manor since 1404.

DYMCHURCH Kent

The Ship
High Street TN29 0NP
Tel (030382) 2122

This is an old brick-built inn facing St Mary's Bay on the coast of the English Channel and is backed by Romney Marsh. It was thus an ideal centre for smugglers at a time when a licence was needed for the export of wool. There was an illicit trade with the continent and smugglers would bring over kegs of brandy and take back bales of wool. *The Ship* had a number of secret stairways and hiding places and several tracks ran inland from this stretch of coast through desolate country to isolated villages and inns on the northern fringe of the marsh. The smugglers knew the country intimately and the traffic in contraband continued well into the 19th c.

The New Hall, where the justices met, is close to the inn and the church. This is where the Lords, Bailiff and Jurats of Romney Marsh hold their annual Grand Leth at Whitsuntide, adjourning afterwards to *The Ship Hotel* for a meal to celebrate the occasion.

ESHER Surrey

*The Bear
High Street KT10 9RQ
Tel (78) 64023

Although the inn was established in 1529 there is little to see of the early structure: the stucco frontage is probably early 19th-c. and the interior has been completely modernised. In coaching days it was an important posting house at the start of the second stage from London to Portsmouth and it had stabling for a hundred horses. Today there are effigy signs in the form of two brown bears on the parapet, described by Charles Harper as 'squatting on their rumps and stroking their stomachs in a manner strongly suggestive of repletion or indigestion'. *The Bear* has associations with Claremont, the nearby house built by Robert Clive in 1786, now a girls' school. In 1816 Claremont became the home of Princess Charlotte when she married Prince Leopold of Saxe-Coburg, though she died a year later. In 1831, the prince became King of the Belgians and in 1832 married the eldest daughter of Louis-Philippe, King of France. During the revolution of 1848, Louis-Philippe fled to England and his son-in-law placed Claremont at his disposal. Some of the French royal household were accommodated at *The Brown Bear*, and in a glass case in the entrance hall are the jackboots worn by the postboy who drove Louis-Philippe to his new home.

FARNHAM Surrey

The William Cobbett
(formerly *The Jolly Farmer*)
Bridge Square GU9 7QR
Tel (0252) 726281

William Cobbett was born here; his father not only kept the inn but also farmed the nearby lands. Cobbett himself wrote that he was 'born in the farmhouse, bred up at the ploughtail, with a smock frock on my back, taking delight in all the pursuits of the farmers, liking their society and having among them my most esteemed friends'. The inn building shows two distinct periods: the right-hand timbered and gabled wing is 16th-c. the rest is 17th-c. The garden behind the inn is described by Cobbett:

> *From my very infancy from the age of six years, when I climbed up the side of a steep sand rock, and there scooped me out a plot of four feet square to make me a garden, and the soil which I carried up in the bosom of my little blue smock frock, I have never lost one particular of my passion for these healthy and rational, heart-warming pursuits.*

The Bush Inn (now **The Bush Hotel**)
The Borough GU9 7NN
Tel (0252) 715237

Dating mainly from the 16th c., and after some rebuilding, the inn became a coaching centre in Georgian times.

FITTLEWORTH West Sussex

The Swan
Lower Street RH20 1EN
Tel (079882) 429

With its origins in the 15th c., *The Swan* became a posting house in the 18th c. It is stone-built and the upper storey is hung with red tiles. The roof was once covered with slabs of Horsham stone but only nine rows remain; the rest is covered with red tiles. The old stables are now used for storage.

John Constable stayed at *The Swan* when he came to Fittleworth on painting expeditions with his brewer namesake. The inn has always attracted artists and students of art. The residents' lounge to the left of the main entrance, sometimes called the 'picture room', has many oil paintings framed as panels around the walls.

In the hall is an old inn sign, *Ye Swanne Inne*, painted about 1900. This was lost for many years but turned up mysteriously at an auction sale in Haslemere and was returned to the inn. The original sign depicted a nude figure with a striking likeness to Queen Victoria, sitting astride a swan. This was soon altered. The face was changed and diaphanous drapes were painted in to transform the figure into a fairy queen. The reverse side shows the swan with a ring round its neck and a frog smoking a pipe in a floating tankard.

FOREST OF DEAN Gloucestershire

The Speech House (THF)
Forest of Dean GL16 7EL
Tel (0594) 22607

Known as the King's Lodge until 1801, *The Speech House* is a square grey-sandstone building of three storeys. It has always been a Verderers' Court and is said to be the oldest court of law in England. The site was previously occupied by a building called Kenesley where the ancient Speech Court was held, but in 1670 a warrant was issued for a new and larger building. This was completed *c.* 1674 and the stables in 1676. A stone lintel believed to be from the stables is now over one of the entrances. Much of the building, including the west front, is in its original state and here, over the entrance to the court room, there is a weathered escutcheon in stone with the date 1680 and the initials C.R.II. The court room with its ancient roof beams is now the hotel dining-room, but it is still officially opened from time to time to deal with matters of 'vert and venison' though this is now little more than a formality. At one time the court could condemn a man to death. Today, the local magistrates normally deal with 'vert' offences and as there are now no deer in the forest, venison offences do not arise. At one time the court room was divided by rails into compartments for the jury and the accused. Today there is only a low raised oak gallery or daïs to remind one of its former function. Speech House was first let as an inn in the 1860s.

FRAMLINGHAM Suffolk

Crown Hotel (THF)
Market Hill IP13 9BQ
Tel (0728) 723521

The Crown, built on the hill leading to the castle, faces the triangular market place of one of Suffolk's most interesting small towns. The inn dates back to the 1550s; however, many of its Tudor features were disguised in the 18th c. The front elevation underwent refacing, and in the interior much of the early craftsmanship was hidden behind plaster and wallpaper. Alterations completed in 1952 revealed much of the original building, including a wealth of oak timbers dating to the early 16th c. Examples of these are to be seen in the bedrooms, the corridor at the front of the inn, the dining-room and in the entrance hall and lounge. Sections of a 16th-c. wattle and daub wall, uncovered in the bar and lounge, are preserved behind glass.

In a local survey published in 1734 (John Kirby's *The Suffolk Traveller*), *The Crown* was noted as one of Framlingham's 'reputable Inns of Entertainment'. It was the calling place for the Ipswich coach until the railway came to East Anglia late in the 19th c. Petty sessions for 33 parishes were held here up to mid-Victorian days. Also, farmers who came to Framlingham's important market met at the inn's corn hall which was erected on the west side of the courtyard in 1847. This space was converted to bedrooms and offices in the 1900s.

FYFIELD Oxfordshire

*The White Hart
High Road OX13 5LW
Tel (0865) 390585

The half-timbered building dates back to the 15th c. When the lord of the manor, Sir John Golafre, died in 1442 he left enough money to build and endow a hospital or chantry house for the poor to be run by a priest who would pray for the soul of the founder. In 1580 the house was purchased by St John's College, Oxford, which already owned land in the vicinity, and was then leased to tenants who kept it as a tavern. They have owned it ever since. The original hall of the hospital was divided into two floors. In 1963 the college restored the hall and the chantry room to their original state.

GLASTONBURY Somerset

The George and Pilgrims
1 High Street BA6 9DD
Tel (0458) 31146

This is one of the few remaining medieval inns in England. It was built by Abbot John de Selwood in 1475 as a *novum*

hospitium for pilgrims to the Benedictine abbey, now in ruins. Many pilgrims received free board and lodging in the abbey hospice; *The Pilgrims Inn*, as it was called before *The George* was added, was for more important guests and visitors. The freestone building has suffered little. There is a central archway and the three-storey bays on either side have mullioned windows, cusped and glazed; though partly filled in with solid stone in the two upper storeys. Above the entrance are three carved shields. One shows the armorial bearings of the abbey, the second bears the arms of Edward IV, and the third still awaits the arms of the patron builder. The initials of this builder, I.S., can be found on shields in the cornices. To the left of the entrance is a stone column which once supported a massive corbel holding a bracket clock and later the sign.

A long flagged and timbered hallway runs through the inn and, to the left of the entrance, massive vertical pieces of hewn timber form the wall between this hallway and the parlour where the abbot received his guests. This room has been enlarged to take in the old abbot's kitchen but the original fire-place has gone. There are, however, many interesting 18th-c. Delft tiles on the wall behind the present fireplace. Among them is one more recent tile: the clue to its identification is clear enough but most people usually take some time to find it.

A spiral staircase leads to the hotel bedrooms and eight of them have 15th-c. features. From one of them Henry VIII is said to have watched the burning of Glastonbury Abbey in 1539.

GLOUCESTER

The New Inn
16 Northgate Street GL1 1SF
Tel (0452) 22177

Edward II was barbarously murdered at Berkeley Castle in 1327; his shrine attracted numerous pilgrims and *The New Inn* was built about 1445 to accommodate them by John Twyning, a monk at the abbey of St Peter.

Overleaf: The Luttrell Arms, Dunster Inset: The Star Inn, Alfriston

The Smith's Arms, Godmanstone

There is no formal frontage to *The New Inn*. It is approached through an archway leading to the old courtyard which has an open gallery at first-floor level. It was on this balcony in Tudor times that the audiences gathered to watch the theatrical performances given by itinerant players in the courtyard below. Lady Jane Grey was proclaimed queen from the gallery on July 9 1552. Nine days later her 'reign' was over and she was imprisoned in the Tower of London.

GODMANSTONE Dorset

The Smith's Arms
Godmanstone DT2 7AQ
Tel (03003) 236

Reputed to be the smallest licensed house in England, *The Smith's Arms* is a 15th-c. building of knapped flints and stone with a deep thatch. A fine sign showing a smith working at an anvil rises above the timber porch. The inn was once a blacksmith's shop and is said

to have been granted a licence by Charles II who stopped to have his horse shod and asked for a drink. 'I have no licence, sire', said the blacksmith, whereupon the king granted him one.

GODSTOW Oxfordshire

★The Trout
195 Godstow Road OX2 8PN
Tel (0865) 54485

This stone-built country inn on the bank of the Thames was originally a hospice attached to the Benedictine nunnery at Godstow, founded by Dame Ediva of Winchester. After the Dissolution of the Monasteries the nunnery became a private house which was destroyed by the Parliamentarian Thomas Fairfax in the Civil War. The hospice was then enlarged to become an inn using building stone from the nunnery ruins.

For years *The Trout* has been a noted meeting place for the members of Oxford University, particularly those

addicted to boating. The interior has
many early features – stone fireplaces,
panelling and fine beams. It was on
the stretch of water seen from the
terrace of *The Trout* that Lewis Carroll
(Charles Lutwidge Dodgson), on the
afternoon of July 4 1862, first told the
story of *Alice in Wonderland* to three
small girls during a river trip.

GORING-ON-THAMES
Oxfordshire

The Miller of Mansfield
High Street RG8 9AW
Tel (04914) 872829

The inn is a creeper-covered building of
flint and brick standing near the bridge
over the Thames. The miller of Mansfield was the first landlord. Accounts
vary as to whether his name was
Richard or John Cockell, and whether
the king who provided the land for the
inn was Henry II or Henry III. The
story, however, is always the same.
Cockell was a miller. He entertained the
king, who had become separated from
his company while hunting in Sher-
wood Forest. Unaware of the identity of
his guest, the miller gave him a pie con-
taining venison from a deer poached in
the forest. He asked the king what was
in the pie. The old ballad continued the
story in these words:

> *'Then I think' quoth our King 'that
> it's venison';*
> *'Eche Foole', quoth Richard, 'full
> that you may see:*
> *Never are we without two or three in
> the roof*
> *Very well fleshed and excellent fat:*
> *But I pray thee say nothing where'er
> thou go;*
> *We would not for two pence the King
> should know.'*

When the company found the king next
morning it soon became obvious to the
miller who his guest had been and he
was filled with anguish. However,
grateful for the hospitality, the king
pardoned him and gave Cockell some
land on which to build the tavern which
became *The Miller of Mansfield*.

GRANTHAM Lincolnshire

The Angel and Royal (THF)
High Street NG31 6PN
Tel (0476) 5816

Known simply as *The Angel* until 1866,
The Angel and Royal is one of the oldest
inns in England. Tradition says that
King John and his retinue lodged
here on February 23 1213 when he held
court in Grantham. The hostelry
appears to have passed to the Knights
Hospitaller *c.* 1312, and the cellars and
a few of the old thick walls may date
from this period. The entrance archway
is believed to have been built in Edward
III's reign. Heads of King Edward and
Queen Phillipa of Hainault are carved
on its hood moulding. The rest of the
front of the inn was built in the 15th c.
Above the gateway is a carved and
gilded angel holding a crown of the con-
ventional leaf design common in church
decoration.

The upper room, above the archway,
known for centuries as the State Room,
or *La Chambre du Roi*, was used by
Richard III on October 19 1483. It was
here that he wrote a letter to the Lord
Chancellor bidding him send the Great
Seal so that he might proclaim the
treachery of his kinsman, the 2nd
Duke of Buckingham. The room has
an oriel window over the gateway and
two other windows, each with carved
stone ceilings. Another window in the
hotel has a carving of a 'pelican of
piety' feeding her young with her own
blood. This has a religious origin and
supports the view that the house may
have been used by pilgrims to the shrine
of St Wulfram, to whom the parish
church is dedicated.

Little is known of the history of *The
Angel* between 1500 and 1700 except
that King Charles I visited the inn on
May 17 1633. In the 18th c. *The Angel*
became one of the foremost coaching
and posting inns on the Great North
Road: hundreds of coaches pulled up
outside every week. There was a good
deal of new building at this period,
including the wings which enclose the
yard.

The Angel continued to prosper even after the advent of the railways in the 19th c. In 1857 the landlord, Richard John Boyall, inserted an announcement in the guide of the Great Northern Railway thanking 'the nobility and the Public generally' for so liberally patronising his hotel. The Prince of Wales (later Edward VII) visited the inn in 1866 when it became The Angel and Royal.

GRASMERE Cumbria

The Swan (THF)
Grasmere LA22 9RF
Tel (09665) 551

A posting house used before the horses began the steady ascent up Dunmail Raise, The Swan was frequently visited by William Wordsworth, who wrote:

> Who does not know the famous Swan
> Object uncouth, and yet our boast,
> For it was painted by the host,
> His own conceit the figure planned,
> 'Twas coloured all by his own hand.

The host referred to was Anthony Wilson, a friend of the poet Coleridge. The inn was used by Sir Walter Scott in 1805.

GRETA BRIDGE Durham

The Morritt Arms
Rokeby DL12 9SE
Tel (0833) 27232

Formerly the 17th-c. George, The Morritt Arms is an old stone-built coaching inn which gave hospitality to Charles Dickens and Hablot Browne when they arrived by coach in deep snow on 31 January, 1838. This was the end of a two-day journey from London on the Carlisle coach. They stayed at The Morritt Arms and continued later by poste-chaise to Barnard Castle.

The present name derives from J. B. S. Morritt, the squire of Rokeby, little more than a mile away. Morritt was a great traveller and his son, who was a connoisseur of pictures, owned the famous painting by Velasquez now in the National Gallery, known as the 'Rokeby

The Feathers, Ludlow

The Swan, Grasmere

Venus'. Morritt the elder was one of the closest friends of Sir Walter Scott.

Greta Bridge has always attracted artists and writers, many of whom have used *The Morritt Arms*. John Sell Cotman, Thomas Girtin and J. M. W. Turner all worked from the inn.

GUILDFORD Surrey

The Angel (THF)
High Street GU1 3DR
Tel (0483) 64555

Originally this was probably a monastic foundation. A vaulted crypt beneath the building consists of three double bays of plain pointed rib-vaulting with two circular columns with plain bases, no capitals, and chamfered ribs. In the 19th c. wall frescoes could be seen in the crypt of *The Angel*, one showing The Flight into Egypt and the other The Crucifixion. From about 1345 the Fyshe Crosse stood in the centre of the High Street. It was erected by the White Friars and was surmounted by a stone flying angel. The inn derived its name and sign from this angel. By 1595 the cross had been removed to ease the traffic jams.

In the 18th c. the inn became a noted coaching house on the Portsmouth Road and coaches left here for London as late as 1840. The words 'Posting House' and 'Livery Stables' remain as lettered signs on the façade above the entrance to the old courtyard.

HAMBLEDON Hampshire

★The Bat and Ball
Broad Halfpenny Down, Hambledon PO8 0SB
Tel (070132) 692

The inn will always be associated with the early years of the game of cricket, for the ground used by Hambledon Club in the 18th c. stretches before it and is marked by a solid piece of grey-granite inscribed:

> *This stone marks the site of the Ground of the Hambledon Cricket Club circa 1750-1797*

The Eight Bells, Hatfield

A carved panel shows two old-style bats and wickets as used in the early game.

The Bat and Ball Inn has changed but the frontage is much as it was when the Hambledon Club was formed in 1750. So is the long-beamed bar. It naturally contains cricketiana but the bats used by the early players are now valued possessions of the Marylebone Cricket Club.

The famous period in the club's history was from 1770 when Richard Nyren was the secretary and also landlord of the inn, which offered 'pavilion facilities'. On 17 June in that year the Hambledon Club defeated an All England team by an innings and 168 runs. The local farmers who watched the matches in those days drank punch at 6d a bottle, a potion 'that would make a cat speak', or maybe ale at 2d a pint 'that would put the soul of three butchers into one weaver'. Nyren's son, John, was also a cricketer and in 1833 wrote *The Young Cricketer's Tutor*.

The sign of The Bat and Ball commemorates Nyren and his players. On one side four cricketers are playing on a pitch with two wickets; on the other side is a portrait of John Nyren.

HATFIELD Hertfordshire

★The Eight Bells
Park Street AL10 5AX
Tel 01-306 6059

This small Georgian alehouse is closely associated with Charles Dickens' *Oliver Twist*. After Bill Sykes had brutally murdered Nancy he reached Hatfield with his dog at nine o'clock at night on his way to St Albans, and turning down 'the hill by the church of this quiet village and, plodding along the little street, crept into a small public house'. This was undoubtedly *The Eight Bells*. It was in the tap room that an antic fellow, half pedlar and half mountebank, after mentioning bloodstains, offered to remove the stain from Sykes' hat.

Dickens' diary records that he stayed in the town with Hablot Browne on December 27 1838.

HAWKSHEAD Cumbria

The Drunken Duck
Barngates, Hawkshead LA22 0NG
Tel (09666) 347

Once known as *The Barngate*, the inn is
some 400 years old and changed its
name in Victorian times. One day the
landlady found six ducks, apparently
dead, sprawled about on the ground
before the front door. She picked them
up, took them to her kitchen, and began
to pluck them. Soon after she had finished they began to show signs of life.
They had, in fact, been drinking beer
which had leaked from a barrel in the
yard. She was horrified and knitted little red jackets for them to wear until
their feathers grew again. It is said that
they recovered. From that day the inn
has been known as *The Drunken Duck*.

HELMSLEY North Yorkshire

The Black Swan (THF)
Market Place YO6 5BJ
Tel (0439) 70466

Dating from the 16th c., *The Black
Swan* was a packhorse inn to which
moorland farmers brought their wool.
The three-storey stone frontage is late
Georgian but many of the thick interior
walls, oak ceiling timbers and fireplaces
are original. The hall was panelled with
Jacobean woodwork from the parish
church when it was being rebuilt between 1849 and 1868. The Tudor stone
doorway to the cellars was brought from
Helmsley Castle.

 The inn, known locally as the Mucky
Duck, has always been a focus for local
life and was an important coaching and
posting house. The annual rent dinners
of the Duncombe estate are held at *The
Black Swan*, when the menu includes
venison from the deer park. It is also a
regular meeting place for the Sunning-
ton Foxhounds.

 In 1947 the inn was enlarged by the
addition of the two-storey Georgian
house next door, and in 1954 the old
half-timbered and red-tiled vicarage
was absorbed into the hostelry.

The Cat and Fiddle, Hinton Admiral

HENLEY-ON-THAMES
Oxfordshire

The Angel on the Bridge
Henley-on-Thames RG9 1BH
Tel (04912) 4977

Henley was the crossing point of the Thames for the main routes north-west from London and consequently has many old inns. *The Angel* is one of them. It may have been built on the site of an ancient hospice called 'The Hermitage', established with monies left for the purpose by John Longland, Bishop of Lincoln in the 14th c. The present building dates from the 17th c. The name no doubt derives from the fact that one of the cellars is built round a complete arch of an earlier Henley bridge. There are three storeys with bays, and a terrace overlooks the river.

The Red Lion
Thameside RG9 1BH
Tel (04912) 2161

With a distinguished history as the main coaching inn of the town, *The Red Lion* dates from the 17th c. It is said to have been built as a hostel for craftsmen and apprentices who built the nearby church of St Mary the Virgin. Charles I is said to have used the inn in 1632 and again, with Prince Rupert, in 1642 during the Civil War. There seems to be some evidence for this since a royal monogram dated 1632, found during building work in 1889, can still be seen in one of the rooms. In the early years of the 18th c. the 1st Duke of Marlborough kept a room at the inn for use on his journeys between London and Blenheim. The present three-storey brick building with its hipped roof is mainly Georgian.

In 1776 Dr Johnson and James Boswell stayed at *The Red Lion*. Royalty used the inn on more than one occasion: George III made frequent visits, once with Queen Charlotte on July 12 1788. When the Prince Regent visited the hotel he is said to have eaten 14 mutton chops for which *The Red Lion's* hostess was famous.

After the Battle of Waterloo, the Duke of Wellington and his Prussian ally, Field-Marshal Blücher, broke their journey at *The Red Lion* when they travelled to Oxford where Blücher was to receive the honour of a Doctorate of Civil Law.

HEREFORD

Green Dragon Hotel (THF)
Broad Street HR4 9BG
Tel (0432) 2506

The Green Dragon, known as *The White Lion* until 1708, appears to have had connections with Hereford Cathedral from an early period. In 1644 it was the property of the Vicars Choral who let it to Barnaby Smythe, baker, for £3 5s. yearly in addition to 'one coople of fatt capons' and 'one coople of fatt henns.' In 1843 it was bought by the famous Bosley family of innkeepers who ran a successful coaching business from here and from the *City Arms Hotel* opposite. They built a large assembly room used from 1845 by the most distinguished and fashionable gentry for Winter Assemblies and on later occasions for concerts, lectures, sales and exhibitions.

The present façade with its pilasters, Corinthian capitals and ornamental balcony, was erected in 1857. In 1931 two houses to the north of *The Green Dragon* were taken in, and the hotel became the largest in Herefordshire. During that period of renovation the ceiling and panelling, dating from *c.* 1600, were discovered in the present Oak Room, as well as a beautiful barge-board *c.* 1500 which is now on the staircase wall of the nearby museum. The panelling in the dining-room came from an immense oak on the Ox Pasture Farm at Marden, 5 miles north of Hereford.

HERNE BAY Kent

The Ship
Central Parade CT6 5HT
Tel (02273) 64638

The building is whitewashed with weatherboarding on the second floor and an outside staircase which was once used for access to the old coroner's court room where inquests were held. The room no longer exists, for the interior has been completely redesigned and the wing on the street corner is now a private house.

The inn dates back to the 17th c., and a slipway opposite which was used in 1666 to load vegetables on to boats for delivery in London after the Great Fire still runs from the road to the shore. It was here that smugglers also landed their goods, using the inn as their meeting place. One night Lieutenant Syden ham Snow, a young exciseman, heard that smugglers were due to land their cargo by *The Ship* and went with his men to arrest them. The smuggling gang proved to be so large that Snow's men fled and left him to cope single-handed. He was shot dead and, despite the fact that a trial was held, no one was convicted due to a lack of witnesses willing to give evidence.

HERTINGFORDBURY
Hertfordshire

White Horse Inn (THF)
Hertford SG14 2LB
Tel (32) 56791

Originally a farmhouse, this building appears to be of 16th-c. half-timbered construction which was altered in the 18th c. (as seen in the brick masking of its façade) and also in the 20th c. During the most recent reconstruction the Gothic tracery of a window was uncovered on the north side of the house, which would date at least that part of the building to the very early 16th or possibly 15th c.

The present inn has many points of interest. The different levels of the ceiling in the entrance lounge tell of the making of this room out of two smaller ones which were separated by a passage. The staircase leading from the lounge is from the days of the Stuart kings in the 1600s. There is also some Jacobean panelling in this lounge, as in other parts of the house.

Enlargements and alterations of Georgian times, evident throughout the building, testify to a thriving trade in coaching days, when traffic on the important Colchester to St Albans road increased yearly.

HIGHAM Kent

*The Sir John Falstaff
Gravesend Road ME3 7NZ
Tel (0634) 77104

Opposite Gad's Hill Place, where Charles Dickens spent the last three years of his life and died, the inn is a 17th-c. building of brick with a hipped roof with dormer windows. Later bay windows have been added to both storeys. The inn is supposed to be on the site where Falstaff caroused with Prince Hal in Shakespeare's *Henry IV*.

In 1676 James Nevison, a highwayman nicknamed 'Swift Nicks' because of his skill with horses, robbed a traveller near the inn. Fearing that he had been recognised he rode to Gravesend, ferried across the river and then rode as fast as he could to York. Arriving on the same day, he changed and met the Lord Mayor of York on the bowling green. When he was later charged with the robbery at Gad's Hill he called on the Lord Mayor as witness that he was in Yorkshire on the day, claiming this as an alibi. This all happened long before Dick Turpin was born, though it is said to be the origin of the story of his ride to York.

HINDON Wiltshire

The Lamb at Hindon
Hindon, Salisbury SP3 6DZ
Tel (042873) 6666

An inn in the 16th c., the present stone building became an important posting house in the 18th and 19th c., catering for the increasing traffic to the West Country. The naturalist and writer W. H. Hudson stayed at *The Lamb* in the spring and summer of 1909 and in *A Shepherd's Life* describes how he

The Tan Hill Inn, Keld

watched the birds around the inn and particularly those that nested close to his window:

> . . . *three pairs of birds – throstle, pied wagtail and flycatcher – breeding in the ivy covering the wall facing the village street. . . There were at least twenty other pairs – sparrows, thrushes, blackbirds, dunnocks, wrens, starlings and swallows. Yet the inn was in the very centre of the village, and being an inn the most frequented and noisiest spot.*

HINTON ADMIRAL Dorset

*The Cat and Fiddle
Lindhurst Road, Hinton BH23 7DQ
Tel (04252) 3088

This is an old thatched inn with lattice windows and walls mainly of whitewashed cob. The two signs suggest that its name is derived from the nursery rhyme. One is in carved oak over the doorway, almost hidden by the deep thatch; the other is a painted post sign.

Both show a cat with a fiddle and a cow jumping over the moon. However, the name is more likely to have been derived from that of Caterine la Fidèle, the name of the owner of the house in the Domesday Book. There was certainly a hospice here in the 11th c., kept by the monks of Christchurch Priory.

In the 18th and 19th c. *The Cat and Fiddle* became a rendezvous for the smugglers of Christchurch Bay and there is a secret hiding place for contraband in one of the old chimneys.

HITCHIN Hertfordshire

The Sun
Sun Street SG5 1AF
Tel (0462) 2092

Probably in existence in the early 16th c., the earliest recorded date for *The Sun* is 1575. Late in the reign of Elizabeth I the Michaelmas Court Leet and the Hitchin justices were meeting in an upper chamber of the inn and early in the 17th c. the Archdeaconry Court

The Bell, Thetford

moved to *The Sun* which then became the leading hostelry in the town.

During the Civil War the inn was used by Parliamentarians: here the freeholders of Hitchin signed their protestation to defend the High Court of Parliament. It became the headquarters for the 3000 soldiers quartered in the town, and the Council of War for Hertfordshire met at the inn and was visited there by leading Parliamentary figures including Cromwell, Hampden and Pym.

For many years after the Restoration *The Sun* was in the doldrums. It was boycotted by the restored nobility and gentry and apart from the townsfolk had little custom. Prosperity, however, returned with the coaching era. In 1741, John Shrimpton established the London–Hitchin and Bedford Coach which inned at *The Sun*, and other routes followed. In 1745 the local militia used it as a recruiting centre and meeting place when preparing to resist the advancing Jacobite forces. At about this time *The Sun* was largely rebuilt with the three-storey frontage of blue brick and the central carriageway seen today. An assembly room was added in 1770. Much of the earlier Elizabethan and Jacobean work still exists behind the Georgian façade.

HOLFORD Somerset

Alfoxton Park Hotel
Holford TA15 1SG
Tel (027874) 211

This Queen Anne country mansion lies well back from the road in some 50 acres of parkland. It has two storeys, a central pediment and a roof with small dormer windows. There is a Tuscan porch approached by a drive. Its chief interest is in its association with William and Dorothy Wordsworth who rented the property in 1797 for £23 a year, including taxes. Coleridge lived nearby at Nether Stowey and they met frequently and formed a close and creative friendship. Together they planned the *Lyrical Ballads*, published in 1798.

HULL North Humberside

*Ye Olde White Harte
Silver Street HU1 1JG
Tel (0482) 26363

Established in 1550, the inn is probably the oldest building in the city. It was restored in 1881 and it is now necessary to see the interior in order to gain a sense of its age. On the ground floor there is much panelling and two large brick fireplaces are inset with Delft tiles. A staircase, the woodwork rippled as the result of a fire, leads to the 'Plotting Parlour', a panelled room with fine early carving over the fireplace.

A panel in the bar tells the story of the events on St George's Day in 1642 when Charles I came to Hull:

> *Whilst Sir John Hotham, the Governor of Hull, was giving a dinner party, he received an intimation from the King that His Majesty, who was then only four miles from the town, deigned to dine with him that day. The Governor, filled with surprise at the unexpected news, retired to his private room (since called The Plotting Room) and sent*

The George, Huntingdon

for Alderman Pelham, the M.P. for the Borough. It was then resolved to close the gates against the King and his followers and a message was despatched to His Majesty informing him of the decision which had been arrived at. The soldiers were called to arms, the bridge drawn up, the gates closed and the inhabitants confined to their houses. About 11 o'clock the King appeared at Beverley Gate but the Governor refused to allow him to enter the walls. The King then called upon the Mayor but that official fell upon his knees and swore that he could not assist, as the gates were guarded by soldiers. Whereupon the King after much strong conversation and proclaiming Hotham a traitor, withdrew to Beverley.

HUNGERFORD Berkshire

The Bear
Charnham Street RG17 0EL
Tel (04886) 2512

At one time *The Black Bear*, this is an old inn which was rebuilt in the 18th c. and has had 19th-c. additions. Henry

VIII is said to have settled the original inn on two of his Queens: first Anne of Cleves and later Catherine Howard.

The inn has associations with William of Orange. One account states that in 1688 when advancing to London to depose James II he stayed at Littlecote House, and arranged to go to *The Bear* for a meal, only to find that it was a rendezvous for his enemies. Another account states that he slept at *The Bear* where he received three emissaries led by Lord Halifax with a message from his father-in-law, the King.

HUNTINGDON Cambridgeshire

The George (THF)
High Street PE18 6AB
Tel (0480) 53096

In existence before Elizabeth I came to the throne, *The George* was sold in 1574 to Henry Cromwell who came from a local brewing family and was probably the grandfather of Oliver Cromwell who was born nearby. Charles I is said to have made the inn his headquarters when he was in Huntingdon in 1645.

The George and Dragon, Hurstbourne Tarrant

The main interest lies in two 17th-c. wings, one of which has an open gallery overlooking the yard. This has a balustrade with late-17th-c. turned balusters and panelled posts supporting the roof. It is supported on wooden posts in the form of columns with moulded capitals and bases. The gallery led to the bedrooms and the outer staircase leading to it is still well preserved.

In the 18th c. and until 1839 regular coaches on the old North Road used the inn on their way to and from London. In 1870 a fire swept the inn, though happily the yard buildings escaped the flames. The present three-storey frontage of yellow brick with rusticated stucco on the ground floor was built after the fire.

HURLEY Berkshire

Ye Olde Bell
High Street SL6 5LX
Tel (062882) 4244

Founded as a hospice attached to the Benedictine Priory of St Mary in 1135, the present two-storey building dates

from the end of the 16th c. It is half-timbered but except at road level the wall timbers are covered with plasterwork. The upper storey, which overhangs slightly, carries several oriel windows, only one of which is original. This may be recognised by its moulded oak mullions and sill. The roof is broken by two gables, one above a timbered porch.

HURSTBOURNE TARRANT
Hampshire

*The George and Dragon
Hurstbourne Tarrant SP11 0AH
Tel (026476) 277

This has probably been an inn since the 11th c. and parts of the present building are very old. The central part of the house may well be 16th-c. or earlier. The deeds date back to 1735 and it was probably at this time that the property was enlarged and the Georgian frontage built.

Hurstbourne Tarrant was known as Up-husband until well into the 19th c. The name was used by William Cobbett who knew the inn well for he often stayed with his friend Mr Blount who lived in a house across the road. 'Blount's cart horse, Tinker, could always be borrowed as a trace horse to help up the hill, and then unhitched at the top he would come back alone and put himself in the stable.'

The two rectangular bays were probably added in Victorian times. One was, in all likelihood, used as a parcels office, for there is a small kneehole desk built in under one window. Above the open fireplace in the bar is the original mail rack with pigeon holes where mail delivered by coach would await collection.

IPSWICH Suffolk

The Great White Horse (THF)
Tavern Street IP1 3AH
Tel (0473) 56558

A large rectangular Georgian building of three storeys, *The Great White Horse* is built on the site of an old timbered inn which is known to have existed in 1518.

The upper storeys are of weathered yellow brick, the ground floor is of rusticated stucco. Above the entrance is an effigy sign described by Dickens in *The Pickwick Papers* as ' . . . a stone statue of some rampacious animal with flowing mane and tail, distantly resembling an insane cart horse . . . '

George II stayed at *The Great White Horse* in 1736, receiving the dignitaries of Ipswich in an upstairs room, despite the fact that he arrived after eleven o'clock at night. Most of the present building dates from the second half of the 18th c. In 1764 the post coaches left the inn every day at 7am and arrived at *The Black Bull* in Bishopsgate, London, at 5pm the same day.

Dickens first stayed at *The Great White Horse* in 1830 when he was sent to Ipswich to report an election for the *Morning Chronicle*. He described the inn in *Pickwick Papers* as having 'labyrinths of uncarpeted passages' in order to lead up to the dramatic story of Mr Pickwick's entry into the wrong bedroom where he encountered the 'middle-aged lady in yellow curl papers'.

ISLEWORTH Middlesex

*The London Apprentice
62 Church Street TW7 6BJ
Tel (01) 560 1915

This is an old Georgian inn on the banks of the Thames; a three-storey brick building with a hipped roof and added bays. The signs depict a young apprentice in 18th-c. costume. Apprentices from the London livery companies used to row up the river for a day's outing and drink ale in the old tavern and the inn has attracted boaters ever since.

KELD Durham

*The Tan Hill Inn
Keld, Richmond DR11 6ED
Tel (0833) 28246

At 1732ft above sea level, *The Tan Hill Inn* is the highest licensed house in England. It is basically a stone cottage with a grey slate roof and a large projecting porch which shelters the entrance from strong winds. It remains much as it was when first built as a rest house for the Tan Hill coal miners and carters who lived in 'bothies' during the week, returning to their homes only at weekends. It was used by farmers fetching coal from the mines and by pedlars travelling between Yorkshire and Northumberland.

KENDAL Cumbria

*The Fleece
Highgate LA9 4TA
Tel (0539) 20163

Established in 1654, the name of the inn indicates the importance of Kendal as the southern gateway to the Lake District when roads were poor and fleeces from the fell sheep were brought by packhorse. The inn is a three-storey building in black and white stucco. The upper storeys overhang and are supported by a row of pillars.

The Woolpack
Stricklandgate LA9 4ND
Tel (0539) 23852

Like *The Fleece*, *The Woolpack* is also 17th-c. and was one of the main centres for the Lakeland wool trade and a place where fell sheep farmers met the wool buyers. It also became an important coaching house and to serve this purpose was largely rebuilt *c.* 1781. The most striking feature is the enormous entrance to the old yard which occupies nearly half the width of the building. It was made to take the wide heavy waggons which replaced packhorses when the roads began to improve towards the end of the 18th c.

KESWICK Cumbria

The George
St John Street CA12 5AZ
Tel (0596) 72076

The oldest inn in Keswick, *The George* dates from Elizabethan times. At this period German miners dug ores of lead and silver in the local Goldscope workings. The miners paid their dues to the queen's officers at *The George*, the main centre of trade. It is said that unscrupulous traders also brought plumbago ore or 'wadd', stolen from the mines of Borrowdale, to be sold at the inn.

In 1715 the Earl of Derwentwater, on his last visit to Keswick, called at the inn for a tankard of ale before riding away to join the rebellion which ended with his death on the Tower Hill scaffold. In the 19th c. it was a noted coaching inn used from time to time by Coleridge, Wordsworth and Southey. The late frontage is Georgian in style.

The Royal Oak (THF)
Station Street CA12 5HH
Tel (0596) 72965

Also Elizabethan in origin, *The Royal Oak* was entirely rebuilt in the 18th c. and became the headquarters of the packhorse trade and, as the roads improved, a posting house and a halting place for stage coaches.

John Teather, the landlord at the beginning of the 19th c., moved to Carlisle and set up a coaching business on the route between Lancaster and Glasgow. In 1837 he was succeeded by his son but railway competition killed the trade and young Teather returned to Keswick where he, in turn, became landlord of *The Royal Oak*.

The hotel was frequented by Coleridge, De Quincey, Shelley, Southey and Wordsworth, and it was here that Sir Walter Scott wrote his *Bridal of Triermain* (1813). Stevenson and Tennyson also stayed at the inn.

KINGS LYNN Norfolk

The Duke's Head (THF)
Tuesday Market Place PE30 1JS
Tel (0553) 4996

Built in 1685 on the site of an older inn called *The Griffin*, *The Duke's Head* was probably named after the Duke of York who, as James II, came to the throne in that year. It was planned by a vintner,

Sir John Turner, to meet a specific need. In those days the town had an important cloth trade and was a flourishing port where ships were built. The merchants who came to trade had to go to the Exchange (now the Customs House) which had been built in 1683. They needed accommodation in the town and Sir John provided it at *The Duke's Head*. It is an imposing three-storey building with a decorative cornice and broken pediment topped by a hipped roof with dormer windows. Contemporary features include a fine stairway and panelled lounge.

KIRKBY STEPHEN Cumbria

The King's Arms
Market Street CA17 4QN
Tel (0930) 71378

This old coaching inn was built at the end of the 17th c. It has three storeys and a Tuscan porch above which two Victorian bay windows have been built out, spoiling the line of the façade. The interior has a number of 18th-c. features including Adam-style doors and a Georgian powder closet.

In the 19th c. *The King's Arms* was an important stop for the mail coaches. In the winter of 1840 a coach left Sedburgh for Kirkby Stephen but when the driver made a call at *The Cross Keys Inn* at Cantley, the horses set off without him, carrying the passengers towards Kirkby Stephen. A male passenger tried to gain the driving seat and grasp the reins but fell off on the icy road. Later, he managed to secure a horse and followed the coach, only to find that the horses had drawn up outside *The King's Arms*. Miraculously, the passengers were safe.

KIRKSTONE PASS Cumbria

The Kirkstone Pass Inn
Kirkstone Pass, Ambleside LA22 9LQ
Tel (09663) 3248

The inn is 1468ft above sea level. The building is probably 17th-c. but did not become an inn until the 19th c. when it

was first known as *The Traveller's Rest*. It is a long, low, whitewashed house of two storeys, slate-roofed; the interior has stone floors and heavy timbering. The exterior is much as it was in the 17th c., but the interior has been modernised.

KNUTSFORD Cheshire

The Royal George
Kings Street WA16 6EE
Tel (0565) 4151

Formerly *The George*, the inn dates from the 14th c. and became a noted coaching inn in the 18th c., after rebuilding. John Byng describes it in his *Torrington Diaries* as it was in 1790:

> This inn is a very good one; the stabling likewise is good, and a wax candle was put into my bedroom . . . I had a diversity of cold viands for supper, as spitchcocked eel, cold fowl, cold lamb, tarts and custards. . . In this inn are built assembly and tea rooms of spacious grandeur, where are held monthly assemblies; at which the maid bragged that none but gentility were admitted.

Knutsford is Mrs Gaskell's *Cranford*, where she was brought up by her aunt. This fine piece of descriptive writing reaches its climax when the chief characters 'were all assembled in the great parlour of The George'. The inn was visited by Princess Victoria on her way to Chatsworth, by Louis Napoleon (later Napoleon III), and by Sir Walter Scott when travelling to Abbotsford.

The Angel
King Street WA16 6HQ
Tel (0565) 52627

Built in Queen Anne style, this old coaching inn is mentioned in Mrs Gaskell's *Cranford*. *The Angel* is named after the mermaid in the ancient coat of arms of the Mere family, Cheshire.

The inn was the business centre of Knutsford life in the 18th c.; auctions were held here at which timber was sold to shipbuilders, and horses were entered for local races at the inn.

LAVENHAM Suffolk

The Swan (THF)
High Street CO10 9QA
Tel (0787) 247477

Lavenham already had a prosperous weaving industry by Tudor times. Merchants who had grown rich on the proceeds built a Guildhall, a Wool Hall and many fine houses. Four of these 15th-c. houses, each one half-timbered with an over-sailing upper storey and steep gables, were united in the 17th c. as *The Swan*. Extensive stabling was provided for the many packhorses which brought wool and cloth from the nearby villages which were noted weaving centres. The plasterwork on the house which forms the corner of Water Street has a Tudor rose and a fleur-de-lys surmounted by a mitre, the emblem of Bishop Blaize, patron saint of wool combers.

The hostelry flourished and in the 18th c. coaching traffic became important and a carriageway led into the courtyard. The 'Lavenham Machine' left

The Swan three days a week for *The Spread Eagle* in Gracechurch Street, London.

Considerable changes were made in the 18th and 19th c. Much of the timbering was covered with plasterwork, open fireplaces were closed and eventually the carriageway was bricked up and the stables were made into a dining-room. Happily, a change of ownership in 1933 led to a major restoration. Timbering was exposed, fireplaces were opened up, and the old carriageway became the entrance hall. In 1962 the 15th-c. Wool Hall was acquired and incorporated. The architect, James Hopwood, created lounges where the old Courtyard had been, and knitted old and new together in harmony by building a large dining hall in Tudor style, using Suffolk craftsmen to shape the timbers.

During World War II, when East Anglia was studded with British and American air bases, many members of Bomber and Fighter Command and the US Army Air Corps frequented *The*

The Swan, Lavenham

Swan. They sometimes wrote their names on the smoke room walls before leaving on important missions and these signatures are still preserved. So is the half gallon glass boot they used for competitive drinking. The record 'swig' is said to have taken a mere 22 seconds!

LEAMINGTON SPA Warwickshire

Clarendon Hotel (THF)
The Parade CV32 4DJ
Tel (0926) 22201

The Clarendon was built specifically as a hotel in 1832 on an entirely virgin site. Situated then on the end of the town, it offered delightful rural views from its upper windows. Visitors had the privilege of walking in the private garden beside the church opposite, then known as the Episcopal Chapel, and in the winter gentlemen could hunt with the Warwickshire and Osbaldeston hounds. By the 1850s hunters could be accommodated in summer at the hotel's own farm. A mews at the back supplied post horses, carriages and phaetons.

Fashionable visitors often frequented the house. In 1835 Lord Frederick, Lady Augusta and Hon. Miss Fitzclarence, the illegitimate children of the reigning monarch, William IV, and the actress, Dorothea Jordan, stayed here. Four years later the king's widow, Queen Adelaide, came to listen to a musical welcome prepared by 1500 children who gathered outside the hotel.

One of the remarkable features of *The Clarendon*, for the days before the introduction of lifts, was the installation on the ground floor of large suites of rooms equipped for the handicapped.

LEDBURY Herefordshire

The Feathers
High Street HR8 1DS
Tel (0531) 2600

Built in 1560, *The Feathers* is heavily timbered with close-set uprights and five gables. Although the main building

The Bull, Long Melford

dates from the 16th c., an additional storey was added later and a new wing was built in the 17th c. For many years the timbers were covered with plaster which was only removed in the 19th c. An assembly room at the back was built on pillars over the courtyard. The coaching trade began in about 1770 and coaches were still calling at the inn a hundred years later.

Ye Olde Talbot
New Street HR8 2OX
Tel (0531) 2963

The gabled frontage, which is timbered with close-set uprights and horizontal bracing, dates from the 17th c., although the inn carries the date 1596. A large canted bay window above the entrance breaks the line of the building. The interior has an oak-panelled room with a fine Jacobean mantelpiece, still much as it was when it was the scene of a clash between Prince Rupert's followers and supporters of Cromwell after the Battle of Ledbury. Two bullet holes in the panelling are said to have been made on this occasion. In the 18th c. *The Talbot* became a coaching house.

LEWES East Sussex

The White Hart
55 High Street BN7 1XE
Tel (07916) 4676

The frontage was built in the 19th c. and the inn gives little appearance of age, but in it are many features which date back to the 16th c. when it was the home of the Pelham family. At this period the wine cellars were used as a dungeon during the persecution of the Protestants. In 1717 the Pelhams moved and their house became an inn.

The first landlord of *The White Hart* was Richard Verral who made it into a coaching establishment and built up such a reputation for good food that many local banquets were held in the inn, including election parties.

In 1761 Tom Paine, who frequently came to *The White Hart* to meet his friends, founded a political discussion club in the inn which came to be known as 'the Headstrong Club' because of the radical views expressed by its members. Tom Paine later described *The White Hart* as 'the cradle of American Independence'.

On October 1 1929 the British Foreign Secretary, Arthur Henderson, and the envoy of the Soviet Republic, M. Dorgalevsky, met in *The White Hart* to discuss the relations between the two countries. An agreement was reached and diplomatic relations were resumed. The Foreign Secretary was criticised for this 'White Hart Treaty', as it was called, and Stanley Baldwin accused him of surrendering to Russian demands 'at a hotel where bitter beer is sold and where cricketers are wont to resort'. 'I think the Foreign Secretary was playing a straight bat very carefully,' he went on, 'but after lunching with the Soviet representative he collapsed.'

The Snowdrop Inn
South Street BN7 2BS
Tel (07916) 2144

The inn stands at the foot of a steep hill. On the eve of Christmas 1836, when the snow was deep on the ground, a storm brought down a mass of snow from the hill above and buried the inhabitants of a group of cottages below. Eight people died and there is a tablet to them in Malling Church. *The Snowdrop Inn* now marks the site of the disaster.

LICHFIELD Staffordshire

The George
Bird Street, WS13 6PW
Tel (05432) 53311

The inn carries a plaque with this information:

> *George Farquhar (1677-1707) lived in the inn on this site whilst as a lieutenant of Grenadiers in 1705 he was recruiting troops in Lichfield. The inn he immortalised in his comedy* The Beaux Stratagem.

No doubt his experiences whilst recruiting were well used in his other play, *The Recruiting Officer*.

The Swan

Bird Street WS13 6PW
Tel (05432) 55851

Dating back to the 17th c., *The Swan* is an old coaching inn. The Lansdown Manuscripts in the British Museum describe a visit of three soldiers, a captain, lieutenant and cornet of horse, to Lichfield in 1634:

> *Thither were we quickly brought to the Lily White Swan in that sweet little City, and no sooner were we lighted than the Cathedral knell called us away to prayers.*

The Swan Inn is mentioned several times by Dr Johnson in his diaries.

LIPHOOK Hampshire

*The Royal Anchor

The Square GU30 7AD
Tel (0428) 722244

Originally a royal hunting lodge used by Edward II in 1310; Samuel Pepys stayed at the inn with his wife in 1668 and the present building would appear to date from about this period. It has two storeys and rooms on the second floor have dormer windows.

The Anchor was a famous posting and coaching house on the Portsmouth road between Hindhead and Petersfield, visited by many famous people. In 1815 the Prince Regent arrived from London and lunched at the inn with the Duke of Wellington and Field-Marshal Blücher after the victory at Waterloo. The inn was used by Lord Nelson on his way to Portsmouth before Trafalgar. Prisoners of war from Portsmouth Docks were chained in the cellars overnight on their journey to prison.

LONDON

*The Black Friar

174 Queen Victoria Street EC4 4DB
Tel (01) 236 5650

A unique public house close to the railway bridge which crosses Queen Victoria Street, *The Black Friar* was built on the site of an old Dominican priory. The style is pure *art nouveau*. The main bar has metal murals showing monks catching fish ('Tomorrow will be Friday'), collecting fruit ('Saturday Afternoon') and singing ('Carols'). The metal lampbrackets and the clock all show *art nouveau* designs with flowing lines, and the window has a stained glass panel of a scene with monks.

The room beyond the main bar is of coloured marble with a mosaic ceiling and the walls are decorated with bronzes and murals by Henry Poole RA, each with its 'turn of the century' motto – 'Don't Advertise it', 'Tell a Gossip', 'Finery is Foolery', 'Haste is Slow', 'Industry is All', 'A Good Thing is Soon Snatched up', 'Wisdom is Rare', and 'Silence is Golden'. The metal light fitments are in the form of monks using yokes to carry buckets.

*The Old Bull and Bush

North End Way NW3 7HE
Tel (01) 455 3686

Built in 1645 as a farmhouse on the edge of Hampstead Heath, the inn was for some years the home of William Hogarth. The 'Bull' derives from the farmhouse, the 'Bush' is a traditional sign for an inn.

In the days when William Pitt, 1st Earl of Chatham, lived at North End House, Hampstead village became a fashionable area, and *The Bull and Bush* was used by such notable figures as Thomas Gainsborough, David Garrick, Sir Joshua Reynolds and Laurence Sterne. Sometimes they would meet there for breakfast. 'Faith,' exclaimed Gainsborough on one such occasion as he poured the new milk into his breakfast cup, 'there is cream upon't – and what a tablecloth! Damask – Dutch damask by the Lord'.

In the 19th c. it was still popular with writers and artists – Charles Lamb, Charles Dickens, Charles Keene and George du Maurier. Then came the Edwardian music hall song – 'Down at the Old Bull and Bush' made famous by Florrie Forde – which made the inn known throughout the country.

*Ye Olde Cheshire Cheese
Wine Office Court, 145 Fleet Street
EC4A 3BY
Tel (01) 353 6170

Approached through an archway on the north side of Fleet Street, the building dates from 1667 and is on the site of an earlier inn destroyed in the Great Fire of London. One hundred years later it must have been well known to Dr Samuel Johnson who lived just round the corner. The cellars of the original tavern are still there and much of the atmosphere of Dr Johnson's day remains. The bar to the right of the entrance has old panelled walls and ceiling, a dog grate, scrubbed tables and a sawdust-covered floor. The window seat is said to have been used by Johnson, and also by Goldsmith who lodged in Wine Office Court. The Chop House itself, to the left of the entrance, is similarly furnished.

Outside the tavern is a summary of its associations:

This lane takes its name from the Excise Office which was here up to 1665. Voltaire came, and, says tradition, Congreve and Pope. Dr. Johnson lived in Gough Square (end of the Court on the left) and finished his great dictionary there in 1775. Oliver Goldsmith lived at No. 6 where he partly wrote The Vicar of Wakefield *and Johnson saved him from eviction by selling the book for him. Here came Johnson's friends – Reynolds, Gibbon, Garrick, Dr. Burney, Boswell and others of the circle. In the nineteenth century came Carlyle, Macaulay, Tennyson, Dickens (who mentions the Court in* A Tale of Two Cities), *Forster, Hood, Thackeray, Cruikshank, Leech and Wilkie Collins. More recently came Mark Twain, Theodore Roosevelt, Conan Doyle, Beerbohm, Chesterton, Dowson, Le Gallienne, Symons, Yeats and a host of others in search of Dr. Johnson and 'The Cheese'.*

The Flask Tavern, London

The Cheshire Cheese is noted for its pies and puddings, particularly for 'Ye Pudding', weighing over half a hundredweight, and made to an old recipe with beefsteak, kidneys, mushrooms, etc. (1st Mon in Oct).

★The City Barge
27 Strand-on-the-Green W4 3PH
Tel (01) 944 2148

On the north side of the Thames east of Kew Bridge, the inn will be found among a row of houses strung along the riverside towpath. It is a 15th-c. tavern of bars with low timbered ceilings and old wooden settles. In the corner of one bar is a late-18th-c. Parliament clock recalling the days when there was a tax on clocks and watches so that people who wished to avoid paying it had to rely on clocks in public places.

Outside *The City Barge* hangs a splendid sign showing the ceremonial craft carrying civic dignitaries down the river. The Corporation Barge of the City of London was once moored at Strand-on-the-Green and when the Lord Mayor and Aldermen used it, they embarked here. The barge was then towed by horses to Hampton Court.

★Ye Olde Cock Tavern
22 Fleet Street EC4Y 1AA
Tel (01) 353 3454

The tavern describes itself as 'famous for food since 1549'. It was originally *The Cock and Bottle* at No 201 and was certainly a flourishing tavern in the 17th c. It closed in 1665 because of the plague, but by 1668 it had reopened, for Samuel Pepys informs us that he went 'by water to the Temple and then to the Cock alehouse and drank and eat a lobster, and sang, and mighty merry'. Samuel Johnson often dined there: the chair he used at *The Old Cock Tavern* is now preserved in his house in Gough Square.

The inn was frequented 200 years later by Alfred Tennyson who often dined there with Edward FitzGerald. It was the subject of his poem 'Will

The Prospect of Whitby, London

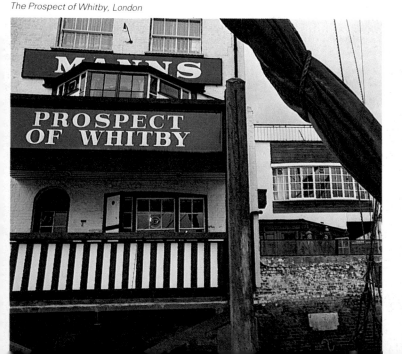

Waterproof's lyrical Monologue made at the Cock', which begins:

> *O Plump head-waiter at the Cock,*
> *To which I most resort,*
> *How goes the time? 'Tis five o'clock.*
> *Go fetch a pint of port:*
> *But let it not be such as that*
> *You set before chance comers,*
> *But such whose father grape grew fat*
> *On Lusitanian summers.*

In 1887 *The Cock Tavern* moved across the street and a few of the furnishings were taken to the new premises, among them a James I chimneypiece. These relics are now in the Dickens Room on the first floor.

*The Dove Inn
19 Upper Mall W6 9TA
Tel (01) 748 5405

Beside the Thames at Hammersmith Pier, *The Dove* is a two-storey building with tiled roof and stuccoed walls, probably part of two 16th-c. buildings at one time used as a single house. It is thought that James Thomson, the poet (who wrote the words for 'Rule Britannia'), occupied a room in the upper storey of No 17 when he came to London in 1725 and that he may have completed his poem 'Winter' here. There are certainly lines in the poem which may have been inspired when watching ice form on the Thames: ' . . . Seized from shore to shore, the whole imprisoned river grows below'. 'Winter' was the first of four poems brought together in 1730 as *The Seasons*.

Later, part of No 17 was set aside as a smoking room for the Duke of Sussex, one of Queen Victoria's uncles, where he could enjoy his 'social tube'. From an iron balcony at behind the inn J. M. W. Turner came to paint scenes of the Thames.

The Flask Tavern
77 Highgate West Hill N6 6BU
Tel (01) 340 3969

On the site of a 15th-c. tavern, the present three-storey building in two types of red brick bears the date 1663 although it was actually built in 1767. The chalybeate springs which made

Hampstead a spa in the 18th c. were discovered near the tavern. The water could be bought in flasks either at the springs or at the tavern – hence its name.

The Flask, together with the other Highgate taverns, used to observe an ancient custom which was usually carried out by the landlord dressed in a black gown and wearing a mask. One of his staff would carry the horns of an ox fixed to a pole. The traveller was then expected to remove his hat, and at the appropriate point in the ceremony to kiss the horns although if ladies were present he was allowed to kiss the girl of his choice instead. H. E. Popham puts forward one theory to account for the custom:

> *. . . the Highgate inns were the resort of graziers bringing cattle from the Midlands to Smithfield . . . these men, wishful of securing accommodation for themselves, formed a kind of fraternity and made it imperative for all who desired to join them to take an oath and kiss the horns – in all probability originally an ox itself.*

The Flask Tavern was much favoured by a number of artists including William Hogarth, George Morland and George Cruikshank.

The George Inn
Borough High Street SE1 1NH
Tel (01) 407 2056

The road which runs south-east from London Bridge was used by pilgrims on their way to Canterbury. In the 16th c. it had a string of inns: *The Spurre, Christopher, Bell, Queene's Head, Tabard, George, Harte* and *King's Head. The George* is now famous as the only remaining galleried inn in London.

Plays were often staged in the yards of these inns, and Shakespeare is said to have acted at *The George*. (The tradition has been revived recently with the performance of Shakespeare here on Saturday afternoons in the summer.) The inns escaped the Great Fire of 1666 but ten years later a fire started in an oil shop early one morning and spread along the street destroying houses and hostelries. *The George* was rebuilt on its former site. Until the 18th c. London Bridge remained the only crossing of the Thames and the main coaching routes coverged on it, fanning out on the southern side to Rochester, Maidstone, Tonbridge and Reigate. The coaches all passed *The George*, which became an important centre.

In the 19th c. *The George Inn* was taken over by the Great Northern Railway Company when coach traffic was dwindling. In 1889 it was partially rebuilt and now only one wing of the earlier structure remains. In this wing the gallery leading to the bedrooms may still be seen. Charles Dickens mentions the inn in *Little Dorrit* (1856-7). In 1937 it was given to the National Trust.

*Jack Straw's Castle
North End Way NW3 7ES
Tel (01) 435 8374

By the White Stone Pond, the highest point in London (440ft), the inn was once known as *The Castle*. It has existed for over 200 years—Samuel Richardson mentions it in *Clarissa*. At one time it appears to have been run by a Mrs Jack Straw, and must surely have gained its present name during her occupation and not, as has been suggested, from Jack Straw, one of the leaders of the peasants' revolt in 1381.

In the 19th c. there were extensive tea gardens and the inn was frequented by Dickens, Thackeray, George du Maurier and Lord Leighton. Dickens persuaded his biographer, John Forster, to join him on one of his trips to Hampstead saying: 'I know a good 'ouse where we can have a red-hot chop for dinner and a glass of wine'. This was *Jack Straw's Castle*. Most of the building is modern, covered with weatherboards and decorated with timber cornices and battlements.

*Ye Olde Mitre
Ely Court, Ely Place EC1N 6SJ
Tel (01) 405 4751

Originally built by Bishop Goodrich in 1546 on part of the garden of the London Palace of the Bishops of Ely, the present building is 18th-c. Built into its façade is a carved and painted stone mitre which appears to be earlier. *The Mitre* is built on Cambridgeshire land and keeps Cambridgeshire hours. The keeping of law and order in Ely Place and Ely Court is the responsibility of beadles. These sanctuary rights are jealously preserved and no policeman enters this territory. At night the lodge gates are locked.

*The Nag's Head
10 James Street WC2E 8BT
Tel (01) 836 4678

This Covent Garden public house is very close to the Royal Opera House and the Theatre Royal, Drury Lane. For years it had a special licence to open at 6.30am for the fruit salesmen of the old fruit and vegetable market. Journalists and publishers from Long Acre, lawyers from the Bow Street courts, businessmen, actors, singers and theatregoers use its bar and restaurant.

*Nell of Old Drury
29 Catherine Street WC2B 5JS
Tel (01) 836 5328

The tavern is opposite the Theatre Royal which opened in 1660. In its early days it was known as *The Lamb* and it is said that a passageway was made between the inn and the theatre which could be used by the theatre staff. Charles II is said to have used this passage when he wished to meet Nell Gwyn. Sheridan who owned the theatre from 1776 may have had an interest in *The Lamb*. His new theatre was opened in 1794 and prospered until it was destroyed by fire in 1809, ending Sheridan's reign as owner and manager.

In the 1820s the name of the inn was changed to *The Sir John Falstaff* and in the 1960s to *The Nell of Old Drury*. The earlier frontage is gone.

*The Prospect of Whitby
Wapping Wall E1 9SP
Tel (01) 481 1095

Built on its Thames-side site at Shadwell in 1520, it was originally

known as *The Devil's Tavern*. It was later named *The Prospect of Whitby* after a Yorkshire sailing vessel from Whitby called *The Prospect* which used to moor at Wapping Wall. It has always been a tavern for sailors and watermen. The building appears to stand on stilts and smugglers are said to have passed up tobacco through trap doors from their boats below the balcony.

Samuel Pepys visited the tavern in the days when the sports were knuckle-fighting and cock-fighting. The execution dock for pirates was nearby and Judge Jeffreys is said to have watched the proceedings from the balcony of the tavern which overhangs Pelican Stairs. He is said to have later hidden at the tavern in the guise of a common sailor when trying to flee the country. He was certainly caught at Wapping before being sent to the Tower to save him from the mobs.

In the 19th c. the tavern was a favourite haunt of J. M. W. Turner, the artist. A more recent regular was A.P. Herbert, the poet.

★The Spaniards Inn
Spaniards Road NW3 7JJ
Tel (01) 455 3276

Built by 1630, *The Spaniards Inn* stands by the toll gate which the highwayman Dick Turpin leapt across on his horse when fleeing from London. The origin of the name is uncertain. Some say that the first landlord was a Spaniard; others that the Spanish Ambassador to James I lived in a house on the site.

The inn has had some notable landlords, among them Giles Thomas who, in 1780, discovered that Kenwood House in the nearby parkland was in danger from Gordon rioters who, in an anti-popery demonstration, had just burned down Lord Mansfield's house. Thomas managed to keep them occupied at *The Spaniards* while the ostler alerted a contingent of the Horse Guards.

The Spaniards was used by Keats and Coleridge when they lived nearby and also by Byron, Shelley and Sir Joshua Reynolds. Early in May 1819 Joseph Severn went to *The Spaniards* with a party of friends which included John Keats. During the evening Keats was found to be missing and was later discovered by Severn lying beneath some trees listening to the song of the nightingales. A few days later he wrote his famous 'Ode to a Nightingale'.

Dickens knew *The Spaniards* well; he used the inn in *The Pickwick Papers*. Mrs Bardell and her friends, determined to have a day out, took the Hampstead coach to *The Spaniards* Tea Gardens where she was arrested by the agents of Dodson and Fogg.

★The Tom Cribb
Panton Street SW1Y 4EA
Tel (01) 839 6536

This public house was called *The Union Arms* until Tom Cribb became the landlord in 1811 after his retirement as 'Champion Boxer of all England'. Although the present building is relatively modern, Tom Cribb is remembered in the name and the interior wall decoration where old prints and bills recall his career as one of the greatest boxers of all time. His first three successful fights were against Jim Maddox, Tom Black and Ikey Pigg. He defeated Jem Belcher in 1809 in 31 rounds and Tom Molyneaux, the negro boxer, in 1810 in 30 rounds and again in 1811 in 8 rounds.

When Tom Cribb took *The Union Arms* he established what was known as 'Tom Cribb's Parlour', which attracted sportsmen, artists, actors and men of letters including John Emery, Lord Byron, William Hazlitt, Thomas Moore and John Reeves, a lawyer at the Board of Trade. In 1837 Renton Nicholson produced this ditty:

> *At the Union Arms in Panton Street,*
> *Lives Tom of vast renown;*
> *A better man, or jollier dog,*
> *Is nowhere in our town.*

> *Your grog, old boy, is excellent*
> *And nowhere do we meet,*
> *More social fun and merriment*
> *Than at yours, in Panton Street.*

*The Trafalgar Tavern
Park Row SE10 9NL
Tel (01) 858 2507

On the Greenwich site once occupied by an alehouse known as *The Old George Inn*, *The Trafalgar Tavern* was built in 1837 to a design by John Kay, the surveyor of Greenwich Hospital. Charles Dickens knew *The Trafalgar* well: it was here that he met Douglas Jerrold, the author and dramatist, for the last time, and he mentions the inn in *Our Mutual Friend*.

In the 1850s *The Trafalgar* was famous for serving 30 fish courses which always included *friture* of whitebait.

In 1883 the Liberals under Gladstone had their last dinner in *The Trafalgar Tavern*. In 1908 the tavern closed and was used for various purposes for some years until its restoration as an inn.

LONG MELFORD Suffolk

The Bull (THF)
Long Melford, Sudbury CO10 9JG
Tel (0787) 78494

Built *c.* 1450 when the town had a flourishing woollen trade manned mainly by immigrant Flemish weavers, *The Bull* started as the house of a wealthy cloth merchant and became an inn *c.* 1570. It is a two-storey, half-timbered building with close-set uprights and tall brick chimneys. The timbered frontage was hidden behind brickwork from early Victorian times and was only uncovered in 1935. The carved uprights and spandrels of the entrance doorway are probably 17th-c. Inside there are many carved and moulded beams, a weaver's gallery and a 16th-c. brickwork hearth. On one of the massive uprights near the door of the lounge is the carved figure of a 'wodewose' or wildman.

In July 1648, during the Civil War, a well-to-do Melford yeoman, Richard Evered, was attacked and killed in the entrance hall of the inn. His body was buried in the nearby churchyard. His

assailant, Roger Greene, was convicted of murder and executed. In coaching days *The Bull* was a posting house on the route from London to Bury St Edmunds.

The Crown Inn
Hall Street CO10 9JL
Tel (0787) 77666

Constructed around fragments of two old houses – a timbered wall and an old cellar, *The Crown* is a 19th-c. building. During the general election of December 1885, it was the scene of a riot. The inn was ransacked, and window frames and furniture were smashed. In the early evening the Riot Act was read by Captain Bence of Kentwell Hall, and soon afterwards fifty soldiers arrived from Bury St Edmunds. The streets were cleared and order restored but only just in time, for *The Crown Inn* had been set on fire by the mob. Fortunately much of the building was saved.

LOWER PEOVER Cheshire

*The Bells of Peover
Lower Peover, Knutsford WA16 9PZ
Tel (056581) 2269

Facing the church of St Oswald, the inn was founded in 1369 as a house for priests. Since then there has been much rebuilding and until the end of the 19th c. the inn was known as *The Warren de Tabley Arms*; the crest of the family with the motto *Tenebo* may still be seen on the north gable. After the death of the third and last baron – John Burne Leicester Warren – in 1895, it became *The Bells of Peover*, not because of any association with the church but from the family name of the licensee – Bell – whose grave is in the churchyard. The next licensee was Victoria Mabel Savage who took a pride during World War II in providing hospitality for officers of the US Army stationed nearby. General Patten stayed at the inn, and General Eisenhower was also entertained here. The inn is now better known as a restaurant.

LUDLOW Shropshire

The Feathers
Bull Ring SY8 1AA
Tel (0584) 2919

Built *c.* 1603 and known to have been an inn in 1656, *The Feathers* has one of the finest timbered façades in England. There are three storeys with bays surmounted by triple gables. The upper storeys overhang and at first-floor level a balustered balcony abuts against the northern bay which projects further than the rest. The timbering, much of which is finely carved, encloses diamond-shaped lozenges of plasterwork on the second storey and cusped lozenges in the shape of a cross on the second. The gables have rounded arches of timberwork.

The interior has some fine early features, particularly plaster ceilings. There is a most interesting panelled room on the first floor. The ceiling carries a moulded centrepiece with the royal arms and supporters of James I surrounded by scrolls of oak, rose, vine and thistle. There is a magnificent carved mantelpiece above the stone fireplace which has an iron fireback with the arms of Elizabeth I. The mantel also has the royal arms and supporters of James I, with the Tudor rose. It is probable that the name *The Feathers* derives from the town's association with the Prince of Wales, who had held court here since medieval times.

MALDON Essex

Blue Boar Hotel (THF)
Silver Street CM9 7QE
Tel (0621) 52681

The Blue Boar was originally a private dwelling which probably belonged to the de Veres, Earls of Oxford, whose heraldic badge was adopted as the inn's sign. The first recorded reference to the house as an inn appears in the Corporation Accounts of 1573. In 1636 the inn was described in John Taylor's *Catalogues of Taverns*, and in 1762 it was noted again in connection with a cockfighting competition. However in the coaching era little is known about *The Blue Boar*, despite its location on the main route between Great Yarmouth and London.

The architectural history of the building is of particular importance, showing periods of construction over 500 years. The oldest remaining section, at the back of the south end of the main block, dates from the 14th c. The adjoining black and white half-timbered wing extending towards the west was added in the 15th c., and most of the main block dates from the following two centuries. The inn's sombre brick façade is an 18th-c. feature to which a graceful Georgian porch was added.

The interior contains Jacobean panelling in the coffee room, some of which was brought from the older back wing, and white-painted pine wainscots of later date in some of the bedrooms. The old south wing has an interesting timber and plaster wall that extends from floor to ceiling and which was probably a screen at the end of a one-storied hall. There are also two 14th-c. doorways with chamfered jambs and 14th-c. ogee heads in this section.

MALTON North Yorkshire

Talbot Hotel (THF)
Yorkersgate YO17 0AJ
Tel (0653) 4031

The town of Malton has for centuries been an important centre for horse-breeding, racing, fox-hunting and coursing. For many generations *The Talbot* (the name for the old English sporting dog) was the gathering place of famous sports enthusiasts.

The house, a severe-looking stone building surrounded by terraced grounds, was built in the early 18th c. and first recorded on an estate map in 1712. It was then known as *The New Talbot*, to distinguish it from the older *Talbot* in the Swine Market.

The new inn became a noted posting house for fashionable Scarborough and here also came the Leeds, Whitby and Scarborough Royal Mail and other coaches. However, its principal memories lie with the celebrated owners, trainers and jockeys who came here to make their plans and to celebrate their victories on the turf. Many noblemen participated in these events, including the Earl of Darlington, the Earl of Carlisle of Castle Howard – who was a cricketer, member of the jockey club and noted gambler – Viscount Chaplin, and Tatton Sykes, the great Sledmere sporting baronet who rode his first race at Malton in 1795.

MARKET HARBOROUGH
Leicestershire

The Three Swans
High Street LE16 7NJ
Tel (0858) 66644

This three-storey 17th-c. building appears to have started as *The Swan*. Later it became a coaching inn. An obituary of William Chapman (1802–74) states that he 'was employed at the Three Swans as helper, post-boy, chaise driver and then ostler for 60 years'.

In the early days of railways the inn declined and had to wait until 1935 to be restored by John Fothergill who continued to run *The Three Swans* until 1952. The most notable feature is the magnificent wrought-iron sign.

MARLBOROUGH Wiltshire

The Castle and Ball (THF)
High Street SN8 1LZ
Tel (0672) 52002

Originally built in Tudor times, the inn was largely rebuilt after two disastrous fires in Marlborough in 1654. The frontage was then set back from the street and a pillared colonnade was created which Pepys described as 'penthouses supported by pillars' when he visited the town in 1668. The inn has three storeys and three gables; the upper storeys are tile-hung. Until 1764

the house was called *The Antelope*. It then became *The Castle and Ball*, possibly a corruption of Castle and Bull, two of the charges in the arms of Marlborough.

In the 17th c. the inn no doubt enjoyed trade resulting from the races held on Barton Down, and in the 18th c. it catered for coaching traffic on the route to fashionable Bath. The Marlborough coach did the journey from the *King's Arms*, Snow Hill, London, in 12 hours, a distance of 74 miles, and passengers would often break the journey and stay a few days at *The Castle and Ball*. It is recorded that the elder Pitt (Earl of Chatham) stayed at the inn during one of his periods of mental illness, and was so demanding that the life of the house revolved around the peevish old man throughout his stay. He even forced the servants to wear the Chatham livery.

The Sun
High Street SN8 1HF
Tel (0672) 52081

This is the oldest surviving inn in the town, having escaped the 17th-c. fires. The frontage has been ruined by the Victorian addition of a lean-to projection and bay windows to the first floor. However the roof with its three dormer windows gives some indication of its age. Inside there are many pre-Elizabethan features including old timbers, some panelling and an old doorway which leads to the cellars.

MARLOW Buckinghamshire

The Compleat Angler Hotel (THF)
Marlow Bridge SL7 1RG
Tel (06284) 4444

The Compleat Angler, bearing the name of Izaak Walton's immortal work on fishing which was published *c.* 1653, has been in existence for about three centuries. At the time that Walton came to Marlow to fish in the pool under the weir, *The Compleat Angler* was just a small riverside inn. The Thames at that point must have been very shallow then, as cattle were driven across it. In place of the present-day bridge there was only a wooden footbridge. The present one, built in 1840, is the single remaining suspension bridge designed by W. Tierney Clark. The only other one he built was in Budapest crossing the Danube; however, that one fell to destruction during World War II.

Although existence of the old inn building has been traced through title deeds only to the early part of the 19th c., it seems that the present bar, part of the restaurant and some of the rooms overlooking the river are remains of the original inn. During the course of this century the hotel has been modernised and extended while still retaining the distinction of former times.

Up to about 1895 *The Compleat Angler*, described as 'a red brick and tile building of picturesque elevation', advertised its coaching facilities. At about the turn of the century, it was bought by Sir Alfred Yarrow and became a fashionable private hotel for the gentry. Sir Alfred, although in his eighties, had a sentimental attachment to his new purchase, for it is on the banks of *The Compleat Angler* that he built, in 1862, the first steam-powered river launch which was to sail the upper reaches of the Thames. After a successful sale he used the profits to set up the Yarrow Shipbuilding Company. This enterprise grew into one of the largest naval shipbuilding yards in the United Kingdom.

The Compleat Angler, Marlow

MERE Wiltshire

The Old Ship
Castle Street BA12 6JE
Tel (0747) 860528

Sir John Coventry, a staunch cavalier who sat in the Long Parliament (1640) erected the building as a private mansion in the early 17th c. It is stone, two storeys high, with a fine archway and a stone slab roof with sky lights. It became an inn in the 18th c., catering for coach traffic on the London to Exeter Road and for racegoers to Mere Down, stabling some of the racehorses. Its fine wrought-iron sign was made by Kingston Avery, a local clockmaker, some time between 1730 and 1763. From it hangs a bunch of gilded grapes (the vintner's sign). Inside the inn are beamed rooms, old stone fireplaces, an elmwood staircase and some early plasterwork ceilings in the bedrooms.

The Talbot
The Square BA12 6DR
Tel (0747) 860427

This inn, opposite *The Old Ship*, was built in the 17th c. when it was known as *The George*. In 1651 Charles II dined at the inn when travelling from Trent to Heale House, north of Salisbury. His party included Colonel Robert Phelips and Miss Juliana Coningsby, with Charles himself disguised as her groom. Fortunately the landlord was known to Phelips as a loyal Royalist, though the identity of the groom was not revealed.

MIDHURST West Sussex

The Spread Eagle
South Street GU29 9NH
Tel (073081) 2211

The inn consists of two buildings of different dates fused into a single unit. The older part is half-timbered and has an overhanging second storey with lattice windows. It dates from 1430. The later part was built in 1650 of stone and brick. It has three main storeys, the third with dormer windows.

The name 'Spread Eagle' derives from the crest of the de Bohuns, medieval Lords of Coudreye (Cowdray). In Elizabethan days the land around was forested – the name Midhurst means 'in the midst of woodlands'. Here the queen and her lords went hunting and returned after the chase to feast at *The Spread Eagle*.

In the 18th c. it became a coaching inn and travellers who spent Christmas there booked a place in the inn for the following Christmas by reserving a pudding. This custom continues, and in the dining room the bookings for Christmas hang from a beam.

MINLEY Hampshire

*The Crown and Cushion
Minley, Camberley GU14 9UA
Tel (0252) 545253

This 17th-c. inn was associated with the adventurer Colonel Blood. In May 1671 he entered the Tower of London with accomplices and they succeeded in stealing the crown and the orb from the Crown Jewels. However, they were pursued and Blood was arrested in the little inn not far from his home. Later, through the good offices of the Duke of Buckingham he was pardoned by Charles II and his estate of £500 a year was restored. The name of the inn derives from this incident.

MORETON-IN-MARSH
Gloucestershire

The White Hart Royal (TIIF)
High Street GL56 0BA
Tel (0608) 50731

Originally half-timbered, most of the present Cotswold-stone building is 16th-c. Charles I slept here in July 1644 while on a journey from Oxford to Evesham. The entrance is now within the old archway used by horses in posting days. A ballroom was added early in the 19th c. and above the entrance is a royal arms carrying the royal coat with red and blue ensigns in the background. This was made for a Moreton tentmaker who undertook government contracts in Victorian times. When he died and the business closed the landlord of *The White Hart* acquired it as a curiosity. The interior of the inn has an interesting old balustered staircase, moulded ceiling beams, and a fine open hearth.

MOULSFORD ON THAMES
Oxfordshire

The Beetle and Wedge
Ferry Lane OX10 9JF
Tel (0491) 381

Ferry lane leads down to the Thames and is probably the point where the old Ridgeway crossed the river. It is a public landing place. It is not surprising, therefore, that there should be an inn here – an attractive brick building now frequented by the owners of river boats. Its main claim to fame, however, is that H. G. Wells made it his Potwell Inn of *The History of Mr Polly*.

A beetle is a heavy wooden mallet which is used for splitting timber.

NEWARK Nottinghamshire

The Clinton Arms
44 Market Place NG24 1EG
Tel (0636) 72299

The present inn was mainly built in the 18th c. on the site of an earlier inn. Lord Byron stayed at the inn in 1806 and 1807 when volumes of his poems were being printed in Newark. Shortly afterwards it became *The Clinton Arms*, taken from the family name of the Earls of Lincoln, who owned part of the borough. In the 19th c. it was a noted posting establishment. The Duke of Wellington stayed at the inn on his way to the Doncaster races and Gladstone addressed the electors of Newark from its balcony during the election of 1832 when he was returned as a Tory member in the first parliament elected under the Reform Bill.

The present building has a pillared colonnade and part of the old yard is now covered-in with a glass roof.

NEWBY BRIDGE Cumbria

The Swan
Newby Bridge, Ulverston LA12 8NB
Tel (0448) 31681

This is a large old coaching house of three main storeys and a slate roof with dormer windows. There is an effigy sign of a white horse above the main entrance. In 1855 Nathaniel Hawthorne described his journey by coach from Milnthorpe Station to *The Swan*, 'which sits low and well sheltered in the lap of the hills – an old fashioned inn where the landlord and his people have a simple and friendly way of dealing with their guests'.

The inn is close to the fine old grey stone bridge of five arches which crosses the River Leven as it leaves Lake Windermere, and has 300 yards of river frontage where there is fishing for brown trout, sea trout and, after July, salmon.

NEWMARKET Suffolk

The Rutland Arms
High Street CB8 8NB
Tel (0638) 4251

Designed by William Kent and built *c.* 1740 on the site of the former Royal Palace of Newmarket, *The Rutland Arms* is a large two-storey building of brick with a decorative cornice and pediments on two sides. The longer frontage faces the main street and has a pillared portico; the shorter side faces east and has a large coaching archway leading to the central yard. For many years the inn was owned by the Duke of Rutland, hence its name.

The Rutland Arms has a sporting tradition. In 1831 Squire George Osbaldstone, a small man only 5ft tall and probably the greatest sportsman of all time, already 45 years of age, announced his intention to beat the record of Dick Turpin's ten-hour ride from London to York. Colonel Charritie bet him one thousand guineas that he would not succeed and a 200-mile round course was pegged out on Newmarket Heath. Despite a fall, Osbaldstone succeeded in covering the course in nine hours. He then went straight to *The Rutland Arms*, took a hot bath, and began an eating and drinking session which lasted nearly to dawn.

There are many stories associated

with the inn. A remarkable one concerns the Earl of Oxford, who once drove a chariot drawn by a team of tame stags from Houghton Hall in Norfolk to Newmarket. Suddenly the stags were pursued by a pack of hounds. The stags reached the courtyard of *The Rutland Arms* and the gates were closed just in time to avoid disaster.

The list of sportsmen who have used the inn is unending and includes Admiral Henry Rous, Fred Archer, Sir Gordon Richards and Steve Donoghue.

NORTHALLERTON
North Yorkshire

Golden Lion Hotel (THF)
Market Place DL7 8PP
Tel (0609) 2404

The Golden Lion was one of the important coaching and posting houses on the old highway from York to Scotland. Its landlords, who kept 60 horses in the stables, supplied the teams for the great coaches travelling throughout the year from Eastern Common, 8 miles to the north, to Thormanby, 15 miles to the south.

Although the house was practically reconstructed in the 18th and early 19th c. during its phase of great prosperity, masonry and Tudor brickwork seen in the cellars confirm that it has been in existence for at least four centuries. One of the interesting features dating from the period of reconstruction is the inn's bar 'mess', that is, the private gathering room for barristers and magistrates who were obliged to be segregated from the general public, while staying at inns, to avoid intimidation or corruption. Records of these mess meetings exist from 1600, the room at *The Golden Lion* apparently being one of the oldest in the country. This bar mess had its own wine cellar and boasted at one time of holding over 250 bottles of port and all the famous vintages of the past century.

In the days of Northallerton's famous Horse Faire, horses were made to run up and down the inn's very long yard to exhibit their paces.

NORTON ST PHILIP Somerset

★The George Inn
The Plain BA3 6LH
Tel (037387) 224

Built as a hospice by the Carthusian priory of Hinton, *The George* also served as a storehouse for the local wool trade – the Carthusian monks were themselves sheep farmers. The original stone building dates from 1397 but a fire destroyed the upper part and only the ground floor remains. The upper storeys were rebuilt, probably about 1500 or a littler earlier. These are half-timbered and overhang, and there are three oriel windows on the first floor. The ground floor has two canted stone bays to the left of the arched entrance. To the right a flight of stone steps leads to a platform and a doorway well above street level. This was probably a loading platform for waggons carrying wool.

The George was used by Cromwell and his men during the Civil War. In 1685, after the Battle of Norton Philip and before Sedgemoor, an attempt was made to kill the Duke of Monmouth when he was staying in the inn. A shot was fired from the street at an upper window but failed to find its mark.

NORWICH Norfolk

★The Bell
Orford Hill NR1 3QB
Tel (0603) 614066

Known in the 16th c. as *The Blue Bell*, some carved oak beams are all that remain of this period. However, there is a good Georgian staircase. The old courtyard has been roofed over and incorporated into the building which now has a relatively modern castellated frontage.

The Bell has always been an inn. Until well into the 1700s it was noted for cockfighting. In the 1750s the landlord was a lively character who could not abide puritanism or authority. During his tenure a 'Hell Fire Club' of local toughs met at the inn and tried to break up meetings held by the Wesleys.

In the 19th c. the house was more law-abiding. It was here that 'the Loyal and Constitutional Club' was founded in 1831. The Duke of Wellington was one of the original members.

The Maid's Head
Wensum Street NR3 1LB
Tel (0603) 28821

Dating from the late 13th c., the inn was originally called *The Molde Fish Tavern*. The name was later changed to *The Mayd's Hedde*.

In the 17th c. the inn became a coaching terminus and as traffic increased in the 18th c. it virtually became the civic centre. Every possible type of local activity took place within the inn – banquets, venison feasts, concerts, lectures and even exhibitions of flowers. In 1742 the first Freemason's Lodge in Norwich was formed at *The Maid's Head* and met in the inn for many years. In 1762 the 'Norwich Machine' left *The Maid's Head* for *The Green Dragon* in Bishopsgate, London, three times a week.

The present building has 'mock Tudor' gables and timbering but inside there is a genuine early fireplace with stone ingle seats and some excellent Jacobean woodwork.

NOTTINGHAM

★The Flying Horse
Poultry NG1 2HW
Tel (0602) 52831

The building carries the date 1483. Perhaps this was the date when it became an inn, because prior to that it was a private house that had been rebuilt in 1392. The inn was largely reconstructed in the 1930s with an impressive gabled frontage, said to be a faithful reproduction of its appearance in Tudor times. It is now best known as a restaurant.

In the 18th c. the inn was the headquarters of the Tory party. In 1818 Thomas Assheton Smith (Master of the Quorn Hunt in 1805) used it as his committee room in an unsuccessful campaign in a parliamentary election. Paul Bedford, the famous vocalist and comedian, stayed at *The Flying Horse* in 1849 when it was kept by William Malpas, a local iron merchant.

The name of the inn is almost certainly derived from an ancient swinging horse which entertained the crowds at medieval fairs. A rider mounted on the horse swung to and fro trying to take a ring from a quintain with a sword.

★The Trip to Jerusalem
Castle Road NG1 6AA
Tel (0602) 43171

The inn boldly claims to be the oldest in England, and carries the date AD 1189. It is said that a group of crusaders encamped outside the castle to refresh themselves at this tavern. Most of the present brick and timber building is only 250 years old but part of the inn has always been a cavern hewn from the brown sandstone of the cliff under the castle.

ODIHAM Hampshire

The George
High Street RG25 1LP
Tel (025671) 2081

In part a Tudor building; much of the original structure remains. The frontage, however, dates from Georgian times when *The George* was an important coaching inn. The dining room has Tudor panelling and a carved Elizabethan chimneypiece which was rescued from Basing House after its siege and destruction by Cromwell's forces during the Civil War. This room was once used as a manorial court and sentenced prisoners could be dealt with on the spot – whipped or taken to the cells below. The cells were used for French prisoners during the Napoleonic Wars. Later the magistrates' court used the inn.

Early in the 19th c. a field at the back of the inn was the scene of many prize fights. Tom Sayers was particularly noted for his prowess there. His last fight with John Camel Heenan, the Benicia Boy, took place on April 17 1860, in a meadow only a few miles from *The George*, both fighters having journeyed to Farnborough from London to escape the police.

ORFORD Suffolk

Crown and Castle Hotel (THF)
Orford IP12 2LJ
Tel (03945) 205

This house was built in 1879 on the site of a much older 17th-c. or possibly 16th-c. tavern or alehouse. Although it was believed that the present building entirely replaced the old premises, during the 1939 alterations two fireplaces as well as moulded ceiling beams belonging to the original house were uncovered in the entrance hall and bar.

The Crown, as it is known locally, became an inn of importance about 150 years ago when the 18th-c. *Orford Hotel*,

now a private house in Church Street, closed. Robert Cooper, landlord of the old hotel, took his business to *The Crown and Castle* in the late 1830s and since then it has remained the principal inn of the town.

Situated on the hill near the keep of Orford Castle built by Henry II in 1165, the inn overlooks the River Ore and the sea. Today it is favoured by anglers, yachtsmen and bird-watchers, but there are also many stories of how it was the haunt of smugglers when Orford was a thriving port.

OSWESTRY Shropshire

The Wynnstay (THF)
Church Street SY11 2SZ
Tel (0691) 5261

Built in the 18th c. to cater for the coaching traffic of the Holyhead Road, the inn was originally called *The Cross Foxes* and became *The Wynnstay Arms* in 1825. The three-storey brick building with a fine four-pillar portico

The Wynnstay, Oswestry

has always been closely associated with the Welsh family of Williams Wynn of Wynnstay. The original name of Cross Foxes referred to the two red foxes in their coat of arms. These can still be seen in a glass lantern light above the portico and also, in the moulded plasterwork of a first-floor lounge which once formed part of a larger assembly hall.

In 1832 the Duchess of Kent and her daughter, Victoria, stayed at *The Wynnstay Arms*. James Knight, the landlord, must have had an anxious time for such large crowds flocked to celebrate the occasion that a woman was killed in the crush. *The Wynnstay* has always been noted for its bowling green, now well over 200 years old.

OUNDLE Northamptonshire

The Talbot
New Street PE8 4EA
Tel (08322) 3261

The inn carries the date 1626 on its sign but it occupies a site where there has been a hostelry since 638. The original, known as *The Tabret*, was attached to a monastery built by Bishop Wilfred. The 17th-c. date marks the complete restoration of the older house. Repairs were done with stone from Fotheringhay Castle, and the panelling in the lounge and the main staircase was from the same source.

The inn is of three storeys and has bays with mullioned windows reaching from ground level to gables on either side of the central archway. The gables are decorated with stone ball finials at both base and apex.

OXFORD

Randolph Hotel (THF)
Beaumont Street
Oxford OX1 2LN
Tel (0865) 47481

Following the visit of the Prince and Princess of Wales to Oxford in 1863, attention was drawn to the absence of a representative hotel, and soon thereafter plans were drawn up for *The Randolph*. William Wilkinson, the architect who contributed a great deal to the layout of north Oxford, designed the building in Gothic style following the example of the University Museum of Natural History and the Union Debating Society. The neo-Gothic style, favoured by George Gilbert Scott and supported by John Ruskin, was the rival to the classical tradition over which much controversy had developed at that time.

In 1866 the hotel was completed and named after the Ashmolean Museum's Randolph Gallery across the street. Despite the architectural contrast of the building, its yellow brickwork was chosen to match the local oolite stone of the Georgian Beaumont Street. The carvings under the bay windows of the vine and hop with animals peeping through are identical to those at the University Museum (the work of William Morris and Edward Burne-Jones). In the late 1940s and early 1950s the hotel was altered by adding new bedrooms and bathrooms within the existing structure, enlarging the lounge, dining-room and ballroom, and constructing a new wing in the original style.

Murals were commissioned for the enlarged ballroom, and an appropriate subject was found in Sir Max Beerbohm's 1911 publication *Zuleika Dobson, or an Oxford Love Story*, which offered a nostalgic glimpse of the town and the life of its students and *alumni*. The artist was Osbert Lancaster, who produced 12 canvases (4ft x 3ft), working in one of the top floor bedrooms of the hotel.

The Randolph has a long list of distinguished visitors, including the Duke of Gloucester, Ferdinand Tsar of Bulgaria, King Farouk and Crown Prince Olaf of Norway. Prime Ministers such as Lord Rosebery, Ramsay MacDonald, Lloyd George and Clement Attlee also visited the hotel, and Max Reinhardt once stayed here while producing *A Midsummer Night's Dream*.

*The Golden Cross
Cornmarket Street OX1 3HA
Tel (0865) 42391

On the site of a building erected by the canons of Osney Abbey and sold to a wine merchant under Richard I, *The Golden Cross* became an inn which retained an ecclesiastical air. About 1390 it was bought by William of Wykeham for New College. Parts of the present building date from the 15th c. Three famous Protestant martyrs stayed at the inn before their trial and execution at the stake: Bishops Latimer and Ridley (1555) and Archbishop Cranmer (1556).

The inn is approached through an old coaching entrance which leads to a cobbled courtyard. Six original oriel windows can be seen. The bay windows on the ground floor are probably 18th-c.

*The Mitre
The High Street OX1 4AG
Tel (0865) 47426

The stone vaulted cellars – now used as wine vaults – suggest an early date for the original building, probably *c.* 1230. The main building today, with three gables, each with an oriel window, dates from the 17th c.

For over 200 years *The Mitre* (now a restaurant) was a coaching inn. In 1671 a 'good coach and able horses' set forth for London 'every Tuesday, Thursday and Saturday. Performed if God permit'.

The inn was for a long period a favourite for members of the university. In the days when 'Town and Gown' were at loggerheads it was the favoured base of the academics.

PENRITH Cumbria

The Gloucester Arms
Great Dockray CA11 7DP
Tel (0768) 62150

According to tradition this was Dockray Hall, the residence (*c.* 1471) of Richard, Duke of Gloucester, who became Richard III. Over the entrance is a carved and emblazoned shield bearing his coat of arms with white boars as supporters.

In 1580 extensive alterations were made. The inn is built of stone, now faced with painted stucco. Inside there are original plaster ceilings with the ducal arms and some 15th-c. panelling.

*The Robin Hood
King Street CA11 7AY
(No telephone)

A plaque on the inn states: 'William Wordsworth stayed here with Raisley Calvert 1794–5.' Raisley was the brother of William Calvert, an old school-fellow of Wordsworth at Hawkshead School. The poet was no doubt concerned for his sick friend who was consumptive. In fact, Wordsworth nursed Raisley for a time in William Calvert's farmhouse, near Keswick. Raisley died in January 1795 and left Wordsworth a legacy of £900.

RIPLEY Surrey

*The Anchor
High Street GU23 6AE
Tel (048643) 2120

A small, many-gabled brick and timber building, *The Anchor* dates in part from the 13th c. It gained a reputation in the 1890s as a port of call when the road between Kingston and Guildford became a popular stretch for cyclists in the days of the 'penny-farthing'. It continued as a haven for cyclists until World War I. Roughly 24 miles from Hyde Park Corner, *The Anchor* made a reasonable afternoon's run for Londoners. The tradition continued into the motorcycle age.

*The Talbot
High Street GU23 6BB
Tel (048643) 3188

Established in 1453, parts of the structure today are original. Claud Duval, the 18th c. highwayman, is said to have used a bedroom at *The Talbot* from which he could escape by way of a chimney and rear door if pursued.

In the 18th c. the inn became a port of call on the coaching road to Portsmouth. It was used, though involuntarily, by Admiral Byng when he was taken to be court-martialled at Portsmouth before he was shot on the quarter deck of the *Monarque* on March 14 1757.

ROCHESTER Kent

*The Crown
2 High Street ME1 1TT
Tel (0634) 45325

Built in 1316 as the Hospital of St Catherine to care for the poor, this is the oldest inn in Rochester. In 1390 it became a manorial inn owned by Simon Potyn who was several times member of parliament for the city. It was in *The Crown Inn* that Henry VIII first set eyes on Anne of Cleves. On September 18 1573, Elizabeth I arrived at the inn and stayed four days. Shakespeare may well have known it for it is said that the inn yard was the one where the flea-bitten carriers tried to borrow a lantern (*Henry IV*, Part 2). In May 1732 William Hogarth went to *The Crown* with his 'four merry companions' where they dined

> . . . *on a dish of soles and flounders with crab sauce, a calf's head stuffed and roasted, the liver fried and other appurtenances minced, all very good and well drest with good small beer and excellent port.*

In 1836 *The Crown* changed hands, and for a time took the name of its new owner, *Wright's*, the inn referred to by Jingle in *The Pickwick Papers*.

Royal Victoria and Bull
16 High Street ME1 1PX
Tel (0634) 46266

Built of brick with a large yard for stabling, this inn was built in the 18th c. as a coaching house on the Dover road. Evidence of the old gallery can be traced in the corridors to the bedrooms.

The inn was often visited by Dickens who is known to have used Room 17. It is *The Bull* of *The Pickwick Papers*

and *The Blue Boar* of *Great Expectations*. Mr Jingle referred to it in *The Pickwick Papers* as 'a good house, nice beds'. The assembly room has a minstrels' gallery which carries the royal arms of Queen Victoria who stayed in *The Bull* as Princess Victoria with her mother, the Duchess of Kent, on November 29 1836, when a storm had damaged the bridge across the Medway.

ROMSEY Hampshire

The White Horse (THF)
Market Place SO5 8ZJ
Tel (0794) 512431

The Georgian brick frontage hides a much earlier building. In the 12th c. there was a guest house for Romsey Abbey on the site. After the Dissolution of the Monasteries it was pulled down and a new inn was built. Its Tudor origins have been revealed over the years. Some years ago a large wall painting in the form of black Tudor roses linked by a curved geometric design was uncovered. The most recent discoveries were in 1961 when Tudor strap-work design paintings were found on the wattle and daub of the timbered walls in the lounge.

In 1776 *The White Horse* was a galleried inn providing 35 beds for guests and stabling for 50 horses. In 1793 the London and the Southampton–Bristol coaches called daily. In 1800 Joseph Phillips, the landlord, enclosed the galleries with windows to keep out the weather and they now form a corridor to the bedrooms.

ROSS-ON-WYE Herefordshire

The Royal Hotel (THF)
Palace Pound HR9 5HZ
Tel (0989) 65105

On the site of a former palace of the Bishops of Hereford overlooking the River Wye, the hotel was built in 1837. It was provided with a large stable yard

The White Horse, Romsey: Tudor wall paintings

to cater for the coaching traffic. In the cellars there is a foundation stone laid by a local Freemason's Lodge.

Charles Dickens met his friend, John Forster, in *The Royal* in 1867 when they discussed the possibility that Dickens might undertake a lecture tour in America. Forster was against it but in the end Dickens went and the tour proved to be a great success. Queen Victoria stayed in the hotel before her accession to the throne, as did Queen Mary when she was Princess Mary of Teck.

RYDE Isle of Wight

Yelf's Hotel (THF)
Union Street PO33 2LG
Tel (0983) 64062

The present hotel probably dates from the early years of the last century, when Ryde was rapidly developing from a mere fishing hamlet to a popular seaside resort. The house was rebuilt in early Victorian times, though the chalk or clunch walls on the ground floor in the kitchen and in the cellar provide evidence of the original construction. Next door to the hotel there is a wine merchant still trading under the name Yelf. The cellars of the two premises were once connected, showing that hotel and wine business were originally a single enterprise.

The 'Writing Room' to the left of the entrance is perhaps the least altered room in the house and most expressive of its original decoration. It has the white-painted, panelled dado which is to be found in many of the rooms, and a door of six panels.

RYE East Sussex

*Ye Olde Bell
33 High Street TN31 7EN
Tel (079 73) 3323

Built in the 15th c., the inn still has some original timbering. It was used by smugglers, particularly by the Hawkhurst Gang in the middle of the 18th c. At one time a tunnel connected it with *The Mermaid Inn*. There was also a door on the first floor which led to the house next door and a 'cupboard' on the ground floor designed so that a smuggler could step into it and use it like a revolving door to gain access to the street.

The George (THF)
High Street TN31 7JP
Tel (07973) 2114

The inn began in the Butchery opposite the Town Hall and moved to a Tudor building on the present site *c.* 1739. A new frontage was built *c.* 1760 when the inn was enlarged, with three storeys, a tiled roof and dormer windows.

The barons of the Cinque Ports were once entertained in the Long Room on the first floor. When a new mayor is elected it has always been customary for him to throw hot pennies from the Long Room balcony to the crowd below. It was a Whig house and when the election results produced a Whig victory it would be celebrated in *The George*.

In 1850 a prodigious banquet of 57 courses was held when Thomas Farncomb, the Lord Mayor of London, visited Rye for the opening of the railway.

The Mermaid
Mermaid Street TN31 7EU
Tel (07973) 3065

This is one of the oldest and finest inns in England. It has escaped modern 'development' and stands in a cobbled street much as it was 500 years ago. The original tavern of wattle and daub was destroyed in 1377, when the French raided Rye, except for the cellars which have a barrel-vaulted ceiling hewn from the rock. In 1420 the inn was rebuilt on the main route leading to the sea through Strand Gate and has been very little changed. It is a half-timbered building with close-set uprights beneath a tiled roof with dormer windows. The upper storey overhangs.

In Elizabethan times it was a centre for feasting and celebration and Elizabeth I herself visited *The Mermaid* when she came to Rye in 1573. The year 1614, when the export of wool was forbidden by law, saw the beginning of 'owling' – the illegal export of wool in exchange for the import of wine, brandy and tobacco. The inn was used as a base for smuggling, which continued well into the 19th c.

The rooms of *The Mermaid* are worth careful study. The reception hall has a fine timbered ceiling supported by a kingpost and there is good oak panelling on the walls. To the left is 'Dr Syn's Lounge' (named after the use of the inn as a setting for Russell Thorndike's *Dr Syn* novels), a room with linenfold panelling and carving which includes the letters J.H.S (*Jesus Hominum Salvator*). This dates from the Reformation when priests took refuge here before crossing the Channel.

The lounge bar has an enormous fireplace, and behind the beam which spans it is a priest's hole. A solid central kingpost supports the ceiling beams and in one corner is a 'secret' stairway leading to a bedroom – a relic of smuggling days. The restaurant has two kingposts, good linenfold panelling and two Caen stone fireplaces.

Notable visitors have included Ford Madox Ford, Hilaire Belloc, Henry James, Ellen Terry and Rupert Brooke.

ST ALBANS Hertfordshire

★The Fighting Cocks
16 Abbey Mill Lane AL3 4HE
Tel (0727) 65830

A small octagonal timber-framed building on a brick base, *The Fighting Cocks* was probably first built early in the 14th c. as an elaborate dovecote. Although it is often described as one of the oldest inns in England it did not become a licensed house until it was rebuilt after a flood in 1599.

In the 17th and 18th c. the inn became a centre for cockfighting. It was renamed *The Fisherman* when the sport was made illegal in 1849, but has since reverted to its earlier name.

Above: The Fighting Cocks, St Albans Below: The Mermaid, Rye

The White Hart
Holywell Hill AL1 1EZ
Tel (0727) 53624

Formerly called *The Hartshorn*, the inn was built in the 15th or early 16th c. It is half-timbered with close-set uprights, a tiled roof and dormer windows. Inside there are fine old beams and one room has a minstrel gallery. When the inn was restored in 1928 some medieval wall paintings were revealed and these are now preserved.

In 1746 Lord Lovat stayed at *The White Hart* with his captors after the Battle of Culloden when he was being taken to the Tower of London. He was later executed for his part in the Jacobite Rising. It was here that Hogarth painted the portrait of Lovat which is now in the National Portrait Gallery.

The White Hart, St Albans

SALISBURY Wiltshire

The King's Arms
St John Street SP1 2SB
Tel (0722) 27629

The building is timber-framed with four storeys of which the upper two overhang. The spaces between the timbers are filled with wattle and daub and one section of the plasterwork has been removed on the frontage to show the material; it is protected by glass.

During the summer of 1651 the landlord allowed the Royalists to use the inn as a secret rendezvous. Lord Wilmot and Henry Peters found asylum at the inn and, with the help of Dr Humphrey Henchman, laid plans for Charles II's escape to France. The inn later became a coaching centre and still has a fine timbered yard entrance.

The Red Lion
Milford Street SP1 2AN
Tel (0722) 23334

Established in the 15th c., *The Red Lion* later became a coaching inn. The three-storey stucco frontage is Georgian. The unusually high coaching entrance leads through a double set of gates (wood and iron) to a fine old yard hung with Virginia creeper. Here is an effigy sign of a red lion and in the entrance hall is a remarkable organ and skeleton clock.

The White Hart (THF)
St John Street SP1 2SD
Tel (0722) 27476

The present building is on the site of an earlier inn. In 1618 when James I came to Sarum to meet Sir Walter Raleigh after the failure of his expedition to Guyana, Sir Walter was already in a lodging in the city. He arrived there on July 27 with his wife, Sir Lewis Studeley and Manourie, a Frenchman who pretended to be knowledgeable about medicine. Fearing the king's early arrival Raleigh realised that he must gain time to prepare a defence, so he feigned sickness and later insanity. By using unguents prepared by Manourie he induced the symptoms of leprosy. Three local physicians were called in and pronounced his condition incurable. At all events, he gained his respite. Each night he worked hard on his *Apology for the Voyage to Guyana* but his exertions after publicly refusing food produced an acute hunger and, according to the chronicler, 'Manourie accordingly procured from The White Hart Inn a leg of mutton and some loaves which Raleigh devoured in secret and thus led his attendants to suppose that he took no kind of sustenance'.

The present brick building was erected *c.* 1800. The frontage is most impressive. A porte-cochère, added in 1820, projects across the pavement. Above this is a balcony with four massive Ionic pillars supporting a pediment at roof level. A large white hart in effigy was placed on this pediment. *The White Hart* is referred to in *Martin Chuzzlewit*.

SANDWICH Kent

★The King's Arms
Strand Street CT13 9HN
Tel (0304) 617330

The inn is of timber construction, stuccoed, with an over-hanging upper storey and tiled roof. There is a finely carved gargoyle on a corner corbel dated 1592. The inn was built when Sandwich was the centre of a flourishing woollen industry run mainly by Huguenot weavers who settled in the town towards the end of the 16th c.

SARRE Kent

★The Crown
Ramsgate Road CT7 0LF
Tel (0843) 81208

Although there was an inn on the site in 1500, the present whitewashed brick building dates from the 17th c. It has always been noted for its cherry brandy. The secret recipe is said to have been handed down from the days when it was brought to the inn by a Huguenot refugee at the end of the 17th c.

Charles Dickens wrote part of *Bleak House* at *The Crown* which is clearly proud of its many well known patrons. On the front wall are boards listing 45 well-known personalities who have visited the inn, among them George Cruikshank, Rudyard Kipling, Lord Carson, Viscount Rothermere, Lady Wyndham and some 30 people associated with the stage, including Ellen Terry, Bransby Williams and Sir Seymour Hicks.

SELBORNE Hampshire

The Queen's
Selborne, Alton GU34 3JJ
Tel (042050) 272

The existing building was erected on the site of an earlier inn called *The Compasses* soon after Queen Victoria came to the throne. *The Compasses* was a low cottage-like building which was certainly known to the famous clergyman-naturalist Gilbert White, who lived close by in The Wakes where he wrote *The Natural History and Antiquities of Selborne*.

In 1830 stormy meetings were held in *The Compasses*, where the small farmers of Selborne met to discuss their grievances with the vicar's warden. There was a serious riot and *The Compasses* was burnt down. The leader of the riot, John Neland, is buried in Selborne churchyard.

The new inn built to replace *The Compasses* was known as *The Queen's Arms*. At this time the village was already attracting many naturalists and carriages were sent from *The Queen's Arms* to Alton to bring visitors on the last stage of their journey.

SHAFTESBURY Dorset

The Grosvenor (THF)
The Commons SP7 8JA
Tel (0747) 2282

With a longer history than its late-Georgian frontage would suggest, *The Grosvenor* is on the site of *The New Inn* which belonged to Shaftesbury Abbey and certainly existed in 1533. By 1626 it had changed its name to *The Red Lion* and by the 18th c. it had become the chief inn of the town. The coaching trade was extensive and *The Red Lion* took a major share.

The inn was largely rebuilt in 1826 and this is possibly when the name changed. It is an impressive three-storey building. The upper storeys overhang and are supported by six massive pillars. There is a central entrance to the old yard and above this, at roof level, a pediment.

The hotel houses the famous Chevy Chase sideboard, carved in solid oak. It tells the story of the Border Battle of Chevy Chase at Otterburn between the Percy ancestor of the Dukes of Northumberland and the Scottish Douglas family. It was carved by Gerrard Robinson of Newcastle between 1857 and 1863, a commission from the Duke of Northumberland.

SHREWSBURY Shropshire

The Lion (THF)
Wyle Cop SY1 1UY
Tel (0743) 53107

The inn stands next door to the old house in which Henry VII lodged when he went to Bosworth field in August 1485. It has a frontage in three parts. In the centre is a small 15th-c. timber-framed building which was rebuilt in 18th-c. Gothic with a 'little open gallery', as Dickens called it, between the first floor windows. On either side are brick-built blocks which were added in the 18th c. The left-hand block has three storeys; the right-hand block four. Here the main entrance has a Tuscan porch which carries an effigy sign of a lion rampant, paw on a bunch of grapes.

In the late 18th c., *The Lion* had become an important social centre, boasting a fine Adam-style assembly room. It has a saucer dome, a minstrel gallery, two carved fireplaces, two large wall mirrors and painted panels with figures on doors and gallery.

Robert Lawrence, who owned *The Lion* at this period, was a leading citizen and a tablet in St Julian's Church refers to his 'unrelenting exertions, for upwards of thirty years, in opening the great road through Wales between the United Kingdoms, as also for establishing the first mail-coach to this town'. Lawrence died in 1806, two years after the Duke of Clarence (afterwards William IV) had stayed for four days at *The Lion*.

In 1830 Madame Tussaud held an exhibition of waxworks in *The Lion*'s assembly room which was lit throughout with coloured lights, and in August 1831 Niccolo Paganini, the great violinist, played there before his departure to the Court of St Petersburg.

In 1836 Charles Dickens stayed at *The Lion* with his illustrator Hablot Browne and used the hotel again 20 years later on one of his provincial reading tours. During the general election of June 1841, Benjamin Disraeli, who was staying at *The Lion*, wrote on the hotel notepaper to the Prime Minister, Sir Robert Peel, as the local results were coming in. In the letter, which hangs in the hall of the hotel, he says: 'The State of the Poll at Shrewsbury this day permits me to renew my fealty to my chief.'

SOUTHAMPTON Hampshire

The Dolphin (THF)
High Street SO9 2DS
Tel (0703) 26178

There was a property called 'le Dolphyn' on this site in 1454, but the first reference to the premises as an inn was in 1548. The landlord at this time was Edward Wilmott, who later became the mayor and MP for Southampton. Sir Humphrey Gilbert dined at the inn in 1582 when planning England's first colonies in the New World.

The Dolphin became important as a meeting place in the early part of the 17th c. In 1635 Archbishop Laud met at the inn with the ecclesiastical commissioners to report on the churchgoing habits of the Puritan community. In 1648 John Taylor, the Water Poet, mentioned the inn as a resting place on the three-day journey from London to Carisbrook in the Isle of Wight where Charles I was imprisoned.

In the 1760s the present Georgian brick façade was added with its remarkable large bow windows on the upper floors. The ground floor, which has a coaching entrance, is rusticated. Above the entrance is a balcony.

Edward Gibbon, who served as a captain in the Hampshire militia from 1759 to 1770, often visited *The Dolphin* where, in 1762, he entertained the City Fathers on the occasion when he was made a Burgess. The assembly room was used as a ballroom from 1785: Jane Austen was a subscriber and attended the balls with her mother and sister.

The façade of *The Dolphin* carries the arms of William IV and Queen Adelaide, indicating royal approval granted in the 1830s. William Makepeace Thackeray was greatly

attracted to the inn, where he wrote part of *Pendennis*. Many years later Queen Victoria stayed here.

During World War I, Field Marshal Earl Haig (then General Haig) used *The Dolphin* as his headquarters when preparing for the embarkation of the British Expeditionary Force for France.

*The Duke of Wellington
Bugle Street SO1 0AH
Tel (0703) 24385

On the site of a 12th-c. stone house (the foundations and cellars of which still remain), the building was owned from 1220 by Benedict Ace, one of the earliest named mayors of Southampton. When the French raided the city in 1338 the house was damaged and had to be partly rebuilt. It was incorporated into the inn *c.* 1490 by a brewer, and was named *Bere House*. The name was changed to *The Duke of Wellington* soon after the Battle of Waterloo.

The present building of three storeys, timber-framed and gabled, with the upper storeys overhanging, was damaged by enemy action in World War II and was restored in 1962–3.

*The Red Lion
55 High Street SO1 0NS
Tel (0703) 333 595

Though altered and restored, *The Red Lion* retains a cellar of the 12th c. and parts of the main building which are 15th c. It is noted for Henry V's Court Room, a half-timbered hall with a fine Tudor fireplace and a gallery, probably used in medieval times by the trade guilds for their meetings and banquets. The hall was used for a treason trial which took place here on August 2 1415. Richard, Earl of Cambridge, Lord Scrope of Masham, and Sir Thomas Grey of Heton, were accused of conspiracy against the life and crown of Henry V. A jury was summoned and the three conspirators were found guilty, condemned to death and executed outside the Bargate nearby.

The façade of *The Red Lion* is not impressive, but no one should be deterred from entering the Court Room.

The Star
High Street SO9 4ZA
Tel (0703) 26199

Most of the present building is Georgian, but old documents suggest there was an inn here in 1601. The vaulted cellars are probably medieval. The inn has four storeys surmounted by a balustraded parapet bearing the royal arms in gilt and colour. A white and gold balcony spans the whole frontage at first-floor level.

SOUTHWELL Nottinghamshire

The Saracen's Head
Market Place NG25 0HE
Tel (0636) 812701

This old timber-framed inn is now fronted with stucco but its age is revealed in the timbered entrance to the yard with its heavy wooden gates. The inn has been used by kings and nobles since the 12th c. The dates when royal visitors have been entertained are listed in the hall:

>   *1194 Richard I*
>   *1213 King John*
>   *1223 and 1258 Henry III*
>   *1281 Edward I*
>   *1331 Edward III*
>   *1395, 1396 and 1398 Richard II*
>   *1646 Charles I*

It was on May 5 1646 at Southwell that Charles I gave himself into the hands of the Scottish Commissioners who handed him over to the Parliamentarians for £400,000. In the 19th c. *The Saracen's Head* was a posting house and housed the Inland Revenue Office.

SOUTH ZEAL Devon

The Oxenham Arms
South Zeal EX20 2JT
Tel (083784) 244

Mentioned in Charles Kingsley's *Westward Ho!*, the inn was at one time the manor house of the Burgoyne family and before that may have been part of a 12th-c. monastery. The present building

is 16th-c. or early-17th-c., solidly built of granite and oak beams, with fine stonework fireplaces.

The inn was well known to the author and playwright, Eden Phillpotts, who described it as 'the stateliest and most ancient abode in the hamlet'.

SPALDING Lincolnshire

The White Hart (THF)
Market Place PE11 1SU
Tel (0775) 5668

The inn dates from 1377, hence the name, from the white hart of Richard II. It was once the priory guesthouse. Rebuilt in the early 16th c., the Tudor work includes moulded beams in the wings that enclose the yard. A fire in 1714 made it necessary to rebuild some parts and the frontage is even later.

In 1586 Mary Queen of Scots is said to have spent a night in the Crown Room on her way to Fotheringhay.

STAFFORD

The Swan
Greengate Street ST16 2JA
Tel (0785) 58142

This 18th-c. coaching inn carries a plaque which refers to its association with George Borrow and his *Romany Rye* (1857). Borrow clearly found it a place of infinite life and bustle. His feeling for *The Swan* was such that he wrote that often in later life, when lonely and melancholy, he recalled the time he spent there and 'never failed to become cheerful from the recollection'. Charles Dickens was less enthusiastic and called it 'the extinct town inn, the Dodo'.

STAMFORD Lincolnshire

The George of Stamford
St Martins PE9 2LP
Tel (0780) 2101

The presence of the inn is announced with a fine gallows sign which spans the road well clear of 'high loads'. Parts of the building (including the crypt) date back to the 11th c. when it was a hospice used by the Knights Hospitaller, but the main block was built in 1597 by Lord Burghley, Lord High Treasurer to Elizabeth I. The centre of the building contains an old chimney stack to be seen in the lounge. The stone fireplace and what appears to be an old bread oven, the whole surmounted by two enormous beams, was uncovered some years ago when a plastered wall was demolished.

A stone arch of this period may be seen to the left of the frontage of the inn which is 18th-c. rebuilding. During this period and well into the 19th c. *The George* was an important coaching inn roughly half-way between London and Edinburgh. Passengers waited for the coaches in the beautifully panelled London Room to the left of the present entrance, once the approach to the courtyard. Many famous guests have used *The George* including Charles I in 1645, the Duke of Cumberland in 1745 as he returned from the victory at Culloden, and Sir Walter Scott on a journey from London to Scotland.

In the entrance hall to the hotel there is a painting of Daniel Lambert, the son of the Keeper of Leicester Prison who, in 1789, when 19 years of age, started to gain weight very rapidly, despite the fact that he ate moderately and drank only water. Moreover he was an active youth and loved sports, particularly coursing and fishing. Eventually he turned his disability to account and started to tour to exhibit his corpulence. He was on tour and seemingly in good health despite his weight of 52 stone 11lb when he died at the age of 39.

STOCKBRIDGE Hampshire

The Grosvenor
High Street SO20 6EU
Tel (026481) 606

This is an early 19th-c. yellow-brick three-storey building with a large central pillared portico supporting a

room on the first floor. It was once owned by Tom Cannon, the jockey and trainer, and in its early days was much used by the racing fraternity. Since then it has been a resort of fishermen who frequent the River Test. It is the headquarters of the exclusive Houghton Club, formed in 1822.

STRATFORD-UPON-AVON
Warwickshire

The Falcon
Chapel Street CV37 6HA
Tel (0789) 5777

Shakespeare would have known *The Falcon* as a private house, for it did not become an inn until 1640. It is a half-timbered building of three storeys set on a stonework foundation, with close-set uprights and horizontal timbers at the floor levels. There are lattice windows on all floors, those on the ground floor built out as canted bays. Until 1930 the timbering was plastered over. The Shakespeare Club was founded in *The Falcon* in 1824.

The Shakespeare (THF)
Chapel Street CV37 6ER
Tel (0789) 294771

Part of the inn may originally have been the Great House of Sir Hugh Clopton (d. 1496) which existed in Shakespeare's day. The other part was a building known as 'the Five Gables'. Together, they have nine gables which form the third storey of the famous half-timbered building. It probably did not become an inn until the 18th c. when it was used by actors.

The White Swan (THF)
Rother Street CV37 6NH
Tel (0789) 297022

Possibly started as the house of a wealthy Stratford merchant *c.* 1450, *The White Swan* has been an inn since Shakespeare's time, when it was known as *The King's Head*. The ancient features are inside the building. Until 1927 the living-room walls of the old house were covered with Jacobean panelling. In that year the panelling was removed, revealing early paintings dating from between 1555 and 1565. They depict the story of Tobias and the Angel from the Apocrypha, but the figures are in 16th-c. costume. The inn has black timbers, fine panelling and a carved Jacobean mantelpiece.

During World War II *The White Swan* was an American Red Cross Centre.

STRETTON Leicestershire

The Ram Jam
Great North Road LE15 7QX
Tel (078081) 361

This is a stone building constructed around a 14th-c. thatched alehouse. A massive beam over the fireplace in the bar has been carbon-dated and is said to be over 1000 years old.

The name *Ram Jam* is unique. The story goes that a passenger from a passing coach promised to divulge a secret to the landlord and his wife. He asserted that he could draw both mild and bitter beer from the same barrel. When the landlord had left for a while, the visitor demonstrated to his wife how the trick could be done. He made a hole in one side of the barrel and told her to ram her thumb into it. Then he made a second hole on the other side and told her to jam her other thumb against that. Having immobilised her, he told her to hang on while he fetched the pegs for the holes. He did not return but departed without paying his bill. The incident is commemorated in the inn sign.

The Ram Jam is associated with the second of two famous fights between Tom Cribb, Champion of England, and Tom Molyneaux, an American negro. Molyneaux slept in the inn and the fight took place at Thirlestone Gap in Leicestershire, about 3½m away, on September 28 1811. For this fight Cribb was trained by a Captain Barclay and he beat Molyneaux, who suffered a broken jaw after eight rounds.

The inn has two contemporary coloured prints of the fight. One was published by Walker & Knight of Cornhill on October 3 1811 and the other by Thomas Tegg of Cheapside on October 16. To produce prints in so short a time, when news was carried by mail coach and the work done by a hand engraver, was no mean achievement.

On the façade of the inn is an old Saxon sundial.

STROOD Kent

★The Crispin and Crispianus
8 London Road ME2 2AA
Tel (0634) 79912

Crispin and Crispianus were Roman brothers who fled to Gaul during the persecution of the Christians by Emperor Diocletian. They settled to make a living as shoemakers but were martyred at Soissons in AD 308. St Crispin is the patron saint of shoemakers.

The inn is said by some to have been founded by a soldier who returned from Agincourt, a battle fought on October 25 1415 – St Crispin's Day. It is much more likely to have been the meeting place for the local guild of shoemakers.

Charley Roberts, who had been an ostler in the coaching inns of Rochester, was once lodged at the inn out of charity. A widower, he made a living by selling lace, thread and tape and on Sundays shaved local labourers. On September 20 1830 he was taken seriously ill and when the doctor came to see the dying man, Roberts revealed the fact that his real name was Charles Parrott Hanger, and that he was a nephew of Colonel George Hanger who had been a close friend of the Prince Regent. He asked the doctor to act as his executor and it was found that this apparently destitute man had left £1000 to a son in Birmingham.

When he was at Gad's Hill Place Charles Dickens often visited the inn, a two-storey brick building with an overhanging weather-boarded upper storey. The inn is now best known as a restaurant.

TAUNTON Somerset

County Hotel (THF)
East Street TA1 3LT
Tel (0823) 87651

The County Hotel is an old inn that has been reconstructed and altered during the last two centuries. In Stuart days it was known as *The Three Cups*, and then in coaching days, when it became the main posting house in the west of England, it adopted the name *The London Inn*, probably since it was the point of departure for the London coaches. Some remains of its one-time vast stables can still be seen at the rear of the house.

The present front and porch date from a reconstruction of 1820, as does the first-floor lounge which was originally the inn's assembly room. A later-built assembly room is now the dining room. Recently (1982) the main bar has undergone major renovation. It is now called the 'Wayvern Bar', which bears the insignia of Somerset and celebrates through its prints, photographs and decoration the glories of Somerset cricket.

TAVISTOCK Devonshire

Bedford Hotel (THF)
Plymouth Road PL19 8BB
Tel (0822) 3221

The Bedford Hotel, opened in 1822, is largely the work of the well-known Plymouth architect John Foulston. Its history, however, dates much further back, to the time when it was part of the famous Tavistock Abbey.

For the first 50 years after the Dissolution of the Monasteries, the Earls of Bedford occupied the house, followed then by Judge John Glanville whose magnificent tomb is in the church opposite the hotel. In 1602 Judge John Maynard, who figured prominently in parliamentary history during the 17th c., was born here and remained a resident until his death in 1690. About 1720 a major rebuilding was started by Jacob Saunders, and it is

during this period that the panelled dining room was added. In 1753 the house was occupied by agents of the Duke of Bedford, and in 1778 Edward Atkyns Bray, poet, writer and vicar of Tavistock, was born in the house.

At the back of the hotel where the larder once was, there is a fine stone porch from *c.* 1500 which led to the infirmary dining hall, now the Unitarian chapel. Standing by the yard at the side of the hotel is the 15th-c. western gateway of the Abbey (Betsy Grimbal's Tower) and south of it, at the end of the Abbey precinct wall, one can see the Still House Tower.

TEWKESBURY Gloucestershire

The Bell
52 Church Street GL20 5SA
Tel (0864) 293293

An Elizabethan building close to the River Avon, *The Bell* may well have started as a monastic hospice in the 13th c.; wall paintings of this period have been found on interior walls. The inn is half-timbered with three storeys and three gables, the upper storeys with a slight overhang. There is a timber porch, and above it hangs a bell-sign on a bracket.

The Bell inn was used in Mrs Craik's *John Halifax, Gentleman*. She first visited Tewkesbury in 1852 and was so impressed with the town that she decided to make it the scene of her fourth book. She learnt that the inn had once been the house of a tanner. This was chosen as the trade of Abel Fletcher, the Quaker mill-owner who became the hero of her story. Mrs Craik visited *The Bell* again shortly before she died in 1887.

The Royal Hop Pole
Church Street GL20 5RT
Tel (0684) 293236

This old coaching inn is best known as the hostelry where Mr Pickwick with his party – Ben Allen, Bob Sawyer and Sam Weller – stopped to dine. The visit is described in *The Pickwick Papers*.

The three-storey Queen Anne inn is built on to an adjoining half-timbered building with dormer windows. At one time a central archway led to the back of the inn; today an impressive Victorian porch supported by iron pillars spans the pavement outside and provides the main entrance. This is surmounted by some intricate ironwork and by the royal arms.

THAME Oxfordshire

The Spread Eagle
Cornmarket OX9 2BW
Tel (084421) 3661

This old red-brick coaching inn is noted for its magnificent wrought-iron sign. It formerly hung from the inn as a bracket sign but when John Fothergill became the landlord in 1922 part of the wall holding the sign was beginning to crumble. He decided to convert the sign into a post sign. The ironwork is early 19th c. and the sign was originally painted by 'Carrington' Partridge. Fothergill was an eccentric figure whose snobbery and excellent cuisine attracted an exclusive clientele of the rich and famous.

THAMES DITTON Surrey

*The Swan
Summer Road KT7 0QQ
Tel (01) 398 1814

This is a black and white Thames-side inn of two storeys with a terrace overlooking the water. William Hone's *Table Book* of 1829 praised the inn for its food:

> *The Swan Inn . . . remarkable for the neatness and comfort of its appearance, and for the still more substantial attraction of its internal accommodation, is kept by Mr. John Lock, a most civil, good-natured and obliging creature; . . . he has a wife absolutely incomparable in the preparation of 'stewed ells' and not to be despised in the art of cooking a good beef-steak, or a mutton chop.*

THETFORD Norfolk

The Bell (THF)
King Street IP24 2AZ
Tel (0842) 4455

Founded in 1493, the inn is timbered with close-set uprights on the ground floor. The upper floor overhangs and there are tall brick chimneys. A massive timber corner post was at one time the official place for posting public proclamations and many old nails used for this purpose are still embedded in the wood. On the northern side of the courtyard there was once an open gallery at first-floor level, but this has been enclosed. It can be traced inside where it now forms a corridor in which traces of the old wattle and daub construction may still be seen. There are Elizabethan wall paintings in some of the bedrooms, discovered when layers of wallpaper were removed. *The Bell* was an important coaching and posting house in the 18th c.

THIRSK North Yorkshire

The Golden Fleece (THF)
Market Place YO7 1LL
Tel (0845) 23108

The building is mainly early-18th-c.; the older part of it is three storeys brick-built with a central entrance and later bay windows at street level. Above the entrance is a wrought-iron bracket sign from which hangs a golden fleece.

Until 1815 the only coaching inn in Thirsk was *The Three Tuns*. In 1815, however, the landlady, Mrs Alice Cass, retired and handed over her coaching trade to her relative, George Blyth, at *The Golden Fleece*. At this time the house was a low, two-storey building, but Blyth bought some adjoining property including a tall brick house with arched windows which provided an access to the rear. It then became a coaching house with stabling for at least 60 horses. Blyth died in 1828 but the trade was carried on by his nephew John Hall and later his son, William. Their portraits hang in the inn.

TONBRIDGE Kent

The Old Chequers
High Street TN9 1AS
Tel (0732) 358957

The present building is mainly 16th-c. but still retains some original timbering dating from 1270. There is a central section of two storeys with dormer windows in the roof, and on either side are gabled wings of three storeys, the upper floors overhanging. The timbered gables have decorative barge-boards. The sign is in the form of a gibbet placed where the original gibbet stood in the 14th c. when the inn was in the centre of the town overlooking the market place and stocks. Wat Tyler's brother is said to have been the last man to have been hanged outside *The Chequers*.

The Rose and Crown (THF)
High Street TN9 1DD
Tel (0732) 357966

Dating from 1695, *The Rose and Crown* became a posting inn in the 18th c. and by 1835 was a coaching centre on the road to Tunbridge Wells and Hastings. The present frontage of three storeys, built of chequered red and blue brick, dates from the early 18th c. There is a fine pillared portico carrying the arms of the Duchess of Kent who came to the hotel with Princess Victoria. The interior still has rooms with old beams and Jacobean panelling.

Tom Pawlet, who became proprietor in 1893, was a keen cricketer. For nearly 50 years he was secretary of the Tonbridge Cricket Club. He played for Kent and at the time of his death in 1923 was manager of the Kent County Cricket Club.

TROUTBECK Cumbria

The Mortal Man
Troutbeck, Windermere LA23 1PL
Tel (09663) 3193

First built in 1689, the present building reveals little evidence of its history. The post sign, however, which stands by the roadside, shows two men, one happy and robust holding a foaming mug, the other thin and pale. This is a modern version of the original alehouse sign which was painted by Julius Caesar Ibbotson in the 18th c. to pay for his stay during a sketching trip. The original verse carried on the sign was:

O mortal man, that lives by bread,
What is it makes thy face so red?
Thou silly fop that looks so pale,
'Tis drinking Tommy Birkett's ale.

UPTON-UPON-SEVERN
Worcestershire

The White Lion
High Street WR8 0UJ
Tel (06846) 2551

Although dating from the 17th c., the inn has a later classical façade with fluted pilasters and a large pillared porch supporting an effigy of a lion rampant. The interior of the inn was reconstructed in 1971.

Sarah Siddons once performed at *The White Lion* with a group of strolling players. In fiction it is the scene of episodes from Henry Fielding's *The History of Tom Jones*, when he brought 'our hero and his redeemed lady into the famous town of Upton and they went directly to that inn which in their eyes presented the fairest appearance in the street, a house of exceedingly good repute'.

A former landlord of *The White Lion* has the distinction of figuring in a popular epitaph:

Beneath this stone in hope of Zion
Doth lie the landlord of 'The Lion';
Resigned unto the heavenly will,
His son keeps on the business still.

WANSFORD Cambridgeshire

The Haycock
London Road PE8 6JA
Tel (0780) 782223

A stone bridge was built in the reign of Edward III to take the Great North Road across the River Nene. *The*

The Haycock, Wansford

Haycock was built close to it as a posting house in 1632 on the site of an earlier inn. A local freestone was used and the roof is of Collyweston slate.

The name Haycock dates from 1636 when a man called Barnaby visited Wansford where the plague was rife. He lay down to sleep on a haycock. John Taylor, the Water Poet, describes the subsequent event:

> *On a haycock sleeping soundly*
> *The river rose and took me roundly*
> *Down the current: people cried,*
> *As along the stream I hied.*
> *'Where away?' quoth they 'From*
>   *Greenland?'*
> *'No; from Wansford Bridge in*
>   *England'.*

The inn carries a painted wall sign of Barnaby on the haycock beneath Wansford bridge.

It is said that Mary Queen of Scots was brought by her jailer, Sir William Fitzwilliam, to the inn on the site of the present *Haycock* on her way to imprisonment at Fotheringhay Castle in 1586. Its later history may be summarised as follows:

1790 Lord Torrington records a visit to the inn in his diary:
This is a nice Inn. Everything clean and in order, the beds and stabling excellent.

1804 *The Haycock* was taken over by a Mr Mallatratt who was 'determined to keep a good larder, with a plentiful supply of tench, pike and other fish'.

1835 On September 2 Princess Victoria and her mother the Duchess of Kent dined and slept in *The Haycock* on their way to visit the Archbishop of York.

1887 Business declined, the licence was surrendered and the inn became a farm.

1899 *The Haycock* became the private residence of Lord Chesham.

1906 Lionel Digby used *The Haycock* as a racing stable with over 100 horses in training.

1928 Lord Fitzwilliam succeeded in securing a licence for *The Haycock* again after fighting the case through three courts to the House of Lords.

WANTAGE Oxfordshire

The Bear
Market Place OX12 8AB
Tel (02357) 66366

This coaching inn was built in the second half of the 18th c. In addition to a post sign, the name is blazoned in gold letters on a blue ground along the parapet; there is an effigy of a bear on the façade and even the stress plates which hold the tie-bars have been cut out in the shape of a bear. In the 1960s the interior was entirely reconstructed but original outside walls remain.

The Berkshire Downs south of Wantage are noted for the training of racehorses and *The Bear* has always been a meeting place for owners and trainers. One day when the trainers were having their annual dinner here they failed to invite the only local lady who owned and trained her own racehorse. In the middle of the dinner she arrived with a lion. There was some consternation at the table, followed by a lively scene. The lion was, in fact, a tame animal but she had made her point.

WELLS Somerset

The Crown
Market Place BA5 2RP
Tel (0749) 73457

This is a late-17th-c. timber-framed building with three storeys and three gables. The early work can best be seen in the courtyard where there are five latticed oriel windows with fine carving on the frames and bracket supports. Below the windows on the first floor are wall panels with the fleur-de-lys. An 18th-c. Wells physician, Claver Morris, records in his diary his weekly visits to the *Crown Coffee House* as it was then called. Here he read the newspapers, met friends, gossiped, transacted business and even saw patients, for it was a common practice in those days for a doctor to attend a coffee house where he could be consulted.

WEST MEON Hampshire

★West Meon Hut
West Meon GU32 1JX
Tel (073086) 291
Restaurant only

In the 17th c. this was a coaching inn known as *The George* where horses were changed on the London to Fareham run. When the Meon Valley railway was authorised in 1897, many Irish workers were brought in and a hut was built behind *The George* and licensed as a drinking place for their use. After the railway was opened in 1903, the name stuck to the premises. The inn is now best known as a restaurant.

WHITCHURCH Hampshire

The White Hart
Newbury Street RG28 7DN
Tel (025 682) 2900

This is a crossroads inn built where the old London to Exeter road crossed the road from Oxford to Southampton. In coaching days travellers who had to change coaches waited in the inn for their connection. As many as 20 coaches a day called at *The White Hart*.

The present building is early 18th c. It is sited on a corner and here the building carries a portico with Ionic pillars, above which stands an effigy sign of a white hart. The dining room has a fine plaster ceiling of *c*. 1700.

Charles Kingsley was a frequent visitor to *The White Hart*, where he stayed when fishing in the Test. He mentions the inn in *Two Years Ago*, and his novel *The Water Babies* was influenced by his fishing experiences in the locality.

WIMBORNE MINSTER Dorset

The King's Head (THF)
The Square BH21 1JA
Tel (0202) 880101

First mentioned in 1726 when it was a two-storey red-brick building with bow windows, by 1848 *The King's Head* was described as a 'Family Hotel, Commercial Inn and Posting House'. At that time it was run by Thomas Laing who used to ride to hounds and entertained the hunt with 'Brown Brandy' for which his house was noted. In 1889 the owner, William Ellis, rebuilt the inn. He added a storey, removed the bow windows, plastered the frontage to resemble stone and built a heavy porch with a balcony from which poll declarations have since been made at parliamentary elections. The painted sign shows Henry VII, whose mother, Margaret Beaufort, was the founder of Wimborne Grammar School.

WINCHESTER Hampshire

*The Eclipse
25 The Square SO23 9ES
Tel (0962) 65676

Sited opposite Winchester Cathedral, and near the church of St Lawrence for which it was once the rectory, *The Eclipse* is a pre-Reformation timbered building, probably 14th-c., which has been well restored. The spandrels of the Tudor-style timber door frame have small painted signs of the earth, moon

and sun 'in eclipse'.

The name of the inn comes from the famous Derby winner Eclipse, a horse bred by the Duke of Northumberland and born during the total eclipse of 1763. Eclipse was never defeated.

The Royal Hotel
21 St Peter Street SO23 8BS
Tel (0962) 3468

Originally built in the 17th c. as a private house, the premises were used from 1794 by a group of nuns who had fled from Brussels in the face of religious persecution following the French Revolution. In 1857 the nunnery moved to Suffolk and the house was acquired by C. W. Benny, who for some years had run a hostelry called *The White Hart* in the High Street. He called the new hotel *The Royal* and it soon became a social centre in the city.

WINDERMERE Cumbria

Old England Hotel (THF)
Bowness on Windermere LA23 3EL
Tel (09662) 2444

The Old England stands in pleasant woodland gardens overlooking Lake Windermere. The principal part of the building was erected in 1820 as a private house; its enlargement and conversion into a hotel took place between 1869 and 1871.

Although the hotel is not of great age, it nurtures a long-standing reputation for its distinguished clientele. Its notable visitors include Kaiser Wilhelm II (1895), and the Queen of Tonga, Salote Tupon (1953).

There is also a long list of sporting people who have stayed at *The Old England*, among them Miss M. B. Carstairs, Lorde Wakefield and Sir Henry Segrave, who was the first man to set a speed of over 100 mph on water. A piece of his speed-boat, *Miss England II*, which broke the record on Lake Windermere on June 13, 1930 while tragically ending Sir Henry's life, was for a time on display in the hotel.

WINDSOR Berkshire

The Castle (THF)
High Street SL4 1LJ
Tel (07535) 51011

The present building was erected as a posting house in the reign of George III with four storeys and an iron balcony at first-floor level. The ground-floor walls are rusticated and a gilded lettered sign proclaims its name on the façade. An early reference to this building is contained in a report of 1778 when the 3rd Duke of St Albans sold the furniture of Nell Gwyn's old house and 'Nell's bed was bought by the landlord of the Castle Inn'. The finest rooms were added when an adjoining private house was incorporated; a number of them have good plasterwork of the period.

The hotel has had hundreds of notable visitors including privy councillors and others arriving for audiences at the castle. In 1814 the Duke of Wellington was entertained at the hotel when he received the freedom of the borough.

The Old House Hotel
Thames Street SL4 1PX
Tel (07535) 61354

On the banks of the Thames by the bridge which separates Windsor and Eton, *The Old House* was built in 1676 by Sir Christopher Wren and was used as his private residence when he was comptroller of the works at Windsor Castle. It is a two-storey brick building with a prominent central pediment.

WINGHAM Kent

The Red Lion
Wingham, Canterbury CT3 1BB
Tel (022772) 217

Dating back to 1286, the inn was originally part of an ecclesiastical building known as Wingham College. It has two storeys, the upper storey overhanging. The hipped roof is broken by a small gable above an oriel window over the main entrance. The diamond panes in this window are set in an iron framework and include some very early red glass. The inn is heavily timbered inside and in the private quarters on the upper floor is a small sessions room where the magistrates' court was held from 1703 until 1886. The old retiring room used by the magistrates is now a bedroom. A Queen Anne staircase leads to this floor.

In the main lounge is an old minute book of 'Her Majesty's Justices of the Peace and Commissioners for Taxes. Monthly and Especial Meetings held at the "Redd Lyon" Wingham, 1703–1712'.

WINTERSLOW Wiltshire

The Pheasant
(formerly *The Winterslow Hut*)
Winterslow, Salisbury SP5 1BN
Tel (0980) 862374

A busy coaching inn in the 18th and early 19th c., the Exeter mail coach stopped here before proceeding to Salisbury. On October 26 1816, as the mail coach 'Quicksilver' drew in to *The Winterslow Hut*, one of the horses was attacked by a lioness which had broken loose from a travelling menagerie bound for Salisbury Fair. A large mastiff sprang to seize the lioness who turned away from the horse, caught the dog and killed it. Eventually a keeper arrived and trapped the lioness. The full account in a contemporary local paper hangs in the hall of the inn together with a print of the scene after James Pollard.

Winterslow has close associations with the critic and essayist William Hazlitt. In 1808 he married and went to live with his wife in a cottage she had inherited in the village. Four years later they moved to London where Hazlitt was a reporter for the *Morning Chronicle*. In 1819 he left the paper and at about the same time left his wife, after a quarrel. He returned to Winterslow and lived in *The Winterslow Hut* where he did some of his best writing. He was visited here by friends, including Charles and Mary Lamb.

WOKINGHAM Berkshire

*Ye Olde Rose Inne
Market Place RG11 1AL
Tel (0734) 780130

The exterior of the building is mainly Georgian with Victorian and later additions. It is said that the original frontage was partially destroyed in an election riot. Inside the inn, however, its 15th-c. origin is revealed in heavy oak beams, panelled rooms and fine stone fireplaces.

Early in the 18th c. John Arbuthnot, John Gay, Alexander Pope and Jonathan Swift met here and spent an afternoon composing a ballad to Molly Mog, the landlord's attractive daughter who was being courted by the young squire of Arborfield. In fact she never married but lived to the age of 70. Here is the last stanza:

> *When she smiles on each guest like her*
> *liquor*
> *Then jealousy sets me agog,*
> *To be sure, she's a bit for the Vicar*
> *And so I shall lose Molly Mog.*

WONERSH Surrey

*The Grantley Arms
Wonersh, Guildford GU5 0PE
Tel (0483) 893351

An old half-timbered manor house with lattice windows built in the 15th c., the inn was named after Baron Grantley of Markenfield, previously Fletcher Norton. Elected Tory MP for Guildford in 1768, he later became Attorney General and Speaker of the House of Commons.

WOODBRIDGE Suffolk

Crown Hotel (THF)
Thorofare IP12 1AD
Tel (03943) 4242

The earliest parts of this building date back four centuries. The best example of its original Tudor structure can be seen in the timbered dining room. In the 18th c. the hotel was enlarged, and

there is some good Georgian panelling and decoration still to be found.

During its early days *The Crown* was used by Suffolk merchants as a centre for barter and exchange. Stores of cloth were brought to the town for export to Flanders, and corn and cheese were brought by wealthy farmers for shipment on coasting vessels to London. The house was also used for assemblies of the various manorial courts held in the town, in particular the Woodbridge-Priory and Woodbridge-Ufford courts. Another reason for *The Crown's* importance was its close proximity to the town's Fair Field, of which the bowling green and the kitchen garden were once a part.

The development of the shipbuilding industry in the 17th c. brought new life and enterprise to the hotel, which then became the rendezvous of shipbuilders and seamen. This was especially the case after the premises were bought by Peter Pett, a member of the famous shipbuilding family who supplied the Royal Navy throughout the 17th c.

YORK North Yorkshire

*The Black Swan
Peasholme Green YO1 2PR
Tel (0904) 25236

This is a timber-framed building with two main gables carrying carved barge-boards. The upper storeys overhang.

The building was originally a private house, the home of William Bowes MP, Lord Mayor of York in 1417, and of his son William Bowes, Lord Mayor of York in 1443, whose grandson, Sir Martin Bowes, was Lord Mayor of London in 1545 and Treasurer of the Mint in the reign of Elizabeth I. In 1683 it became the home of Edward Thompson MP, Lord Mayor of York in that year, and of his daughter, Henrietta Wolfe, and her husband, parents of General James Wolfe of Quebec, who lived in the house as a child from 1724 to 1726. Subsequently the house became an inn, and although much restored retains its original character.

Index of Inns

People